Thinking Strategies

Exercises for Mental Fitness

Larry E. Wood

A SPECTRUM BOOK

PRENTICE-HALL, INC.
Englewood Cliffs, New Jersey 07632

Library of Congress Cataloging-in-Publication Data

Wood, Larry E.
    Thinking strategies

    "A Spectrum Book."
    Includes index.
    1. Thought and thinking—Problems, exercises, etc.
2. Problem Solving—Problems, exercises, etc.
BF455.W596   1985   153.4'2   85-17017
ISBN 0-13-918129-6

10 9 8 7 6 5 4 3 2 1

Printed in the United States of America

Contents

Preface

Thinking is such a natural part of us that we seldom stop and reflect on it. In the twelve long years of formal schooling, knowledge is often equated with basic facts. Ordinarily, little time is spent consciously developing thinking skills. Rather, it is assumed by teachers that students will acquire these skills through the study of specific subjects, typically mathematics. This may be sufficient for the small number of students who continue mathematics through high school, but for the vast majority who do not continue their math training, there are few opportunities to develop fully their cognitive skills.

I believe that these skills are vital for success in all areas of study. A critical analysis of a play or a poem can require as much logical reasoning as proving a theorem in geometry. I believe that training in cognitive skills should be part of every person's education, and this book represents one way of going about developing a set of those skills relevant to solving problems.

In this book I will explore the heuristic side of problem solving through exercises consisting primarily of games and puzzles, or what are sometimes referred to as "brain-teasers." I have taken this approach for the following reasons:

1. Definitions and explanations are just not enough. It is more practical to learn the ideas by interacting with problems than by reading a lot of useful tips which simply exhort one to "Do this" or "Do that."

2. Puzzles and games draw on common, everyday experience and therefore do not require background in a specific field of study. Thus, we can concentrate on strategies involved in problem solving, without being hampered by a lack of specific knowledge. Furthermore, I am interested in de-

veloping general problem-solving skills applicable to all areas of intellectual endeavor.

3. I believe that everyone understands and remembers best what they discover for themselves. Thus, my objective is to provide the experiences which will lead the student to discover how to use general problem-solving skills in a wide variety of problem situations.

It has been said many times that you only get out of something what you are prepared to put into it. For this book, that is the Golden Rule. Each problem that appears here has been carefully selected for a definite reason—to illustrate, through its solution, specific problem-solving skills. To fully appreciate these skills (and hence the purpose of the problem) it is important that you *stop reading and try to solve the problem* when asked to do so. No one expects that you will always be successful, and in fact no one will know whether you peeked at the solution or not. So I strongly recommend that if you want to benefit fully from the discussions that follow each problem, you should be an active reader. This means, lay down the text when prompted and try the problem on your own. At the end of each chapter a number of exercise problems are given. These are provided for reinforcement and practice and we believe that the following law holds:

> Your growth in problem-solving ability is directly related to the amount of agony you are willing to endure while searching for a solution to the exercise problems.

Thus, if you do not follow this advice, it would be possible to read the entire text without significantly improving your problem-solving ability.

Reluctantly, at the end of the book I have provided solutions to the practice problems. I am reluctant because it is my experience that we all tend toward mental laziness. Therefore, when the answer is provided, we are less willing to put forth the time and energy to see a problem through to the end. Because of this I have tried to provide more than just the answer, but also a description or an outline of how you could obtain the answer using a particular method or combination of the methods discussed in the book.

This book is a result of a joint venture that began several years ago with my good friend and colleague, Donald T. Piele, at the University of Wisconsin-Parkside. The original ideas and the selection of discussion problems are at least as much his as mine.

This book simply would not have happened in the absence of the very productive relationship we enjoyed while I was at "Parkside." I shall always be deeply grateful for his influence on my professional endeavors (of which this book is a part), but most of all I shall value his friendship.

1

Getting
Organized

As was indicated in the preface, the purpose of this book is to help you learn to be a better problem-solver. Because life consists of a series of problems to be solved, success in life is obviously related to your ability to find adequate solutions to problems. Although this book is not guaranteed to make you an instant success, a careful study of its principles should provide you with useful skills to approach problem-solving with greater confidence.

Plagued by a history of failure, many people develop a "one shot" approach to problem solving. If the solution to a problem isn't immediately obvious, they give up in despair. Thus, the first goal of this book is to convince you (just in case you're one of those people I've been talking about) that there is hope after all. Furthermore, I show you that even when your first analysis leaves you uncertain of the next step, the battle is far from lost—if you're willing to persist. One of the major differences between successful and unsuccessful problem solvers is that successful problem solvers are more persistent.

GET ORGANIZED—MAKE A PLAN

The first step in solving any problem is to organize and formulate a plan to guide your efforts. Otherwise, you may waste time going around in circles. A plan allows you to decide what actions to take and the best order in which to take them.

Analysis of a problem

To analyze a problem, it is useful to separate it into three components—the *givens*, the *goal*, and the *operations*. The goal is the reason there is a problem; it is the result that needs to be attained. The givens are the basic information or facts provided in the statement of the problem. The operations are the actions that are possible to get from the givens to the goal.

As an example, consider an everyday situation such as your car running out of gas on the way to work. Your goal is to get to work—on time, you hope. The givens are: You're two miles north of your place of work, you car is out of gas, and you're one mile south of a gas station. Some of the possible operations might be walk to work, try to hitch a ride to work, walk back to the gas station, or try to hitch a ride back to the gas station. In order to solve the problem, you must decide what actions to take and the order in which to take them.

As another example, assume that you're a cycling enthusiast and you're taking a tour on a bike trail. You want to know your average speed over the first fifty miles, which you've covered in four hours. For this problem, *stop reading the text and write the givens, the goal, and the operations.* The givens are that you've traveled fifty miles in four hours, and the relationship that the average speed (or "rate," as it's often called) equals the distance divided by time. This familiar relationship is not stated explicitly, but it is assumed that you understand it. The goal is to determine the average speed. It is reached through the operations of substituting values (distance and time) into the relationship and carrying out the division. Most people could solve the problem from their working knowledge of the relationships without going through the formalities of an equation (*e.g.*, $r = d/t$), but it does illustrate the process.

Poor memory?—more organization

Solving problems requires the manipulation and integration of information. This information may be explicitly stated in the problem, or it may be assumed to be part of our common knowledge. Furthermore, in the process of solving a problem, new information is often generated. Thus, one of the biggest obstacles in problem solving can be organizing and recording the relevant information. Because the number of facts and conditions usually exceeds our capacity to hold them easily in mind, we must turn to using symbols and to organizing information on paper.

One of the most common methods of symbolizing information for problem solving is to use letters of the alphabet to stand for the objects and variables in the problem. For example, instead of saying that International Business Machines Corporation and American

Telephone and Telegraph Corporation are involved in a joint venture, we talk about a joint venture between IBM and AT&T. Likewise, in the formula for the bicycle problem ($r = d/t$), "r" symbolizes rate, "d" symbolizes distance, and "t" symbolizes time. One of the advantages of using symbols is that it provides a way to concisely represent the problem. That is one reason for using arithmetic symbols (+, -, ×, ÷, and =). Consider the difference between the statement "three hundred twenty-six plus five hundred eighteen divided by thirty plus fifty-five equals eighty-three point one three three" and its symbolic representation, $326 + 518 ÷ 30 + 55 = 83.133$.

After people learn to use symbols to represent problems, they can still encounter difficulties translating the words and numbers from a problem into concise symbolic relationships. For example, consider the following problem:

If Tom is twice as old as Howard will be when Jack is as old as Tom is now, who is oldest, next oldest, and youngest?

Stop reading and try to solve the problem. This problem can be solved by translating the words into symbols and inferring the relationships between them. The critical elements are the ages of the three boys. Even though the problem is stated in one sentence, that one statement contains so much information that it all runs together. Therefore, each part must be analyzed separately and represented with symbols. Mathematicians tend to favor letters such as X, Y, and Z, but it is often more useful to use a letter that is related to the object it represents, such as the first letter of the object's name.

The first part of the problem "If Tom is twice as old as Howard will be . . ." implies that Tom is older than Howard and it can be symbolized as $T > H$ (just in case you don't remember, $>$ means "greater than," and $<$ means "less than"). The next part ". . . when Jack is as old as Tom is now . . ." implies that Tom is also older than Jack and it can be symbolized as $T > J$.

Now that we know the relationship between Tom and Howard and between Tom and Jack, we need to establish the relationship between Howard and Jack to finish the problem. This can be found indirectly by a closer comparison of each of their ages with Tom's present age. The statement says that when Jack reaches Tom's present age (when $T = J$—second part of the statement), then Tom's present age will be twice that of Howard ($T = 2H$—first part of the statement). Thus we can see that at a particular point in time, Tom will be twice as old as Howard. From these two relationships, we can then conclude that Jack must be older than Howard (J > H). Putting it all together, we then have T > J and J > H, so Tom is oldest, Jack is next, and Howard is the youngest. As you can see, it is very important to establish the relationships between the elements or components in the problem.

As another example, consider the Fishing Problem in Figure 1.1. *Stop reading and try to solve the problem.*

Figure 1.1. Fishing Problem.

Al, Dick, Jack, and Tom were counting up the results of a day's fishing: (1) Tom had caught more than Jack; (2) Between them, Al and Dick had caught just as many as Jack and Tom; (3) Al and Tom had not caught as many as Dick and Jack. Who had caught the most, second most, third most, and least?

As before, it is important to analyze the givens by providing symbols for the elements and establishing the relationships among them. Let's use the first letters of each of the names as symbols. From statement 1, we can determine the relationship, T > J. From the second statement, we can infer A + D = T + J. Finally, from the third statement, we can see that A + T < D + J.

From here, the problem can be solved by some sound reasoning. *If you have not solved the problem yet, stop and give it another try!*

First notice that the difference between statements 2 and 3 is that Tom and Dick traded places. This resulted in upsetting the balance in favor of Dick and Jack. If you imagined this happening on a playground teeter-totter, what would that tell you about the relative weights of Dick and Tom? It would mean that Dick was larger than Tom. Thus you can conclude that D > T, or that Dick caught more fish than Tom.

Next, consider the second relationship once again, and ask about the relative number of fish for Al and Jack. Because we now know that Dick caught more than Tom, what would have to be the relationship between Al and Jack in order for statement 2 to be true? Hopefully, you can see that J > A, or that Jack caught more fish than Al. We now have enough information to answer the problem. Dick caught more than Tom, Tom caught more than Jack, and Jack caught more than Al.

The second advantage of symbols is that we can represent unknown as well as known information in a problem. Especially in an arithmetic problem like the cycling problem, it is a considerable savings to be able to represent the relationships between distance, rate, and time as a formula with symbols such as $r = d/t$. Then we can substitute the givens into the formula, and the expression becomes $r = 50 \text{ miles}/4 \text{ hr} = 12.5$ miles per hour.

Representing and organizing problem information

For more complex problems than those we have discussed so far, it is essential to develop a way to organize and record all the information that is generated. For example, suppose you were asked to determine how many different ways there are to throw a "7" with a pair of dice. One way to solve the problem is to simply list the possibilities in a table and count them (see Table 1.1). There are six ways to throw a "7." The table provides a way to organize the information (the outcomes of the dice must sum to 7), which can then be used to solve the problem. It is important to find a systematic way of organizing the information, such as starting with a "1" on the first die and counting the values on the second die that give "7." Then go to a "2" on the first die, etc. This way you can be certain that you have accounted for all the possibilities without repeating or missing any.

Table 1.1. The ways
a 7 can be thrown
from a pair of dice.

DICE		TOTAL
1	2	
1	6	7
2	5	7
3	4	7
4	3	7
5	2	7
6	1	7

Figure 1.2. Overworked Librarian Problem.

Our local librarian has been very busy. On Monday she catalogued only some of the new books received. Tuesday she received as many new books as were uncatalogued on Monday, and she catalogued ten. Wednesday she received twelve more than on Monday and catalogued as many as she had done on that day. Three times as many books arrived on Thursday as she had catalogued on Wednesday, and eight were catalogued. On Friday, six books arrived and twelve fewer were catalogued than were received on Wednesday. On Saturday she was able to catalogue the outstanding sixteen books because the library was closed. How many books arrived on Monday?

Drawing pictures, constructing tables, and making graphs are other ways that good problem solvers use to better understand the problem. The result is that facts and relationships are transformed into images and symbols that summarize the problem in a visual form, making it easier to understand. As an additional benefit, just the conscious effort involved in making the transformation of words into images and symbols contributes to a better understanding of the problem.

For another example, consider the Overworked Librarian Problem in Figure 1.2. *Stop reading and begin to solve this problem* by organizing the information by days.

There is enough information in this problem to require the use of paper and pencil. One way to use them in organizing the problem is to construct a table like Table 1.2. *Stop reading and fill out this table if you haven't already done something similar to it.*

Table 1.2. *Beginning Table for the Overworked Librarian Problem.*

	BOOKS RECEIVED	BOOKS CATALOGUED
Monday		
Tuesday		
Wednesday		
Thursday		
Friday		
Saturday		

The goal of this problem is to find the number of books that were received on Monday. Because it is unknown at the beginning, we can symbolize it with the letter "R" for "received." The number of books catalogued on Monday is also unknown—call this number "C" for "catalogued." The books received and catalogued on the remaining days can then be recorded in terms of their relationships to R and C or by actual numbers where they are given. For example, consider the third sentence in the problem. The phrase "Tuesday she received as many new books as were uncatalogued on Monday" can be represented as the difference between R (those received on Monday) and C (those catalogued on Monday), or R - C. The entire problem can be recorded similarly as shown in Table 1.3.

Table 1.3. Information represented for the Overworked Librarian Problem.

	BOOKS RECEIVED	BOOKS CATALOGUED
Monday	R	C
Tuesday	R - C	10
Wednesday	R + 12	C
Thursday	3C	8
Friday	6	R
Saturday		16

The total number of books received is the sum of the numbers in the left-hand column, and the total number of books catalogued is the sum of the numbers in the right-hand column. An important relationship to recognize is that because all books received were catalogued by the end of the week, the two-column totals must be equal. In completing the solution, you can imagine two equal piles of books on either side of a large balance, one representing those received and one representing those catalogued. Because some of the quantities still are unknown, you can simplify the relationship by adding or subtracting equal quantities on each side even if you don't know the actual numbers.

Looking at both columns, you can see that R books were received on Monday and R books were catalogued on Friday, so you can remove both of them. Likewise, the total catalogued on Monday and Wednesday (C + C) balances 2C out of the 3C received

Table 1.4. Balancing the books received and catalogued in the Overworked Librarian Problem.

	BOOKS RECEIVED	BOOKS CATALOGUED
Monday	~~R~~	~~C~~
Tuesday	R - ~~C~~	~~10~~
Wednesday	R + ~~12~~	~~C~~
Thursday	~~3~~C	~~8~~
Friday	~~6~~	~~R~~
Saturday		16
Total	2R	16

on Thursday, so 2C can be removed from both sides leaving C books received on Thursday. Next, the remaining C books received on Thursday cancel the -C from R - C received on Tuesday (C - C = 0). Finally, you can remove the 12 known books from the left side and 12 of the 34 known books from the right side. This leaves 2R books on the left side and 16 books on the right side. The results of these operations are shown in Table 1.4. If 2R = 16, then R = 8 and we now know that 8 books were received on Monday.

It is rare when one problem-solving strategy is all that is needed to solve a problem. Most often a combination of several is needed. The next example shows that organizing the search for a solution is almost always necessary for success, but not sufficient. Inference and trial and error, covered in the next two chapters, are problem-solving strategies that can also be useful in most problems. The Dominoes Problem, found in Figure 1.3, illustrates this point. *Stop reading and try to solve this problem.*

5	1	4	6	0	3	3	5
6	5	4	6	2	2	4	0
4	5	4	5	0	0	2	5
6	2	1	3	3	6	3	0
4	2	3	5	0	1	6	6
0	1	4	1	4	1	5	6
2	1	3	2	0	3	2	1

Figure 1.3. Dominoes Problem.

A full set of dominoes (28 pieces from "00" to "66") was placed on a table in a rectangular pattern with some dominoes facing vertically and some horizontally, but all are touching at least one other domino. Someone copied down the positions of each number but did not draw the outlines of the dominoes. A domino is a small black rectangle made of material such as wood or plastic. There is a line dividing the domino in half, and each half has a number of dots on it. The number of dots can range from 0 to 6. In the problem, the numbers represent the number of dots on each half of a domino. Therefore, the task is to determine which numbers go together to form the separate dominoes. Can you replace the outlines?

One way to begin this problem is to make a systematic list of all 28 dominoes as in Table 1.5. Then, as each one is found in the problem, it can be crossed off the list to help keep track of ones that haven't been found yet.

Table 1.5. Method to record dominoes found.

00						
01	11					
02	12	22				
03	13	23	33			
04	14	24	34	44		
05	15	25	35	45	55	
06	16	26	36	46	56	66

The place to begin is to find pairs that *must* go together to form dominoes because they appear together only once in the problem. The easiest ones to identify are those than can occur in only one combination. For example, 00 and 55 both occur only once, whereas 65 or 14 may occur instead of 56 or 41. Also, those pairs of numbers are adjacent to one another four different times. As dominoes become identified, not only are we closer to the goal, but it becomes much easier to pick out the remaining ones. For example, after 55 has been identified, then there is only one possibility for 45; once this has been determined, there is only one possibility left for 44. This information can be recorded as shown in Figure 1.4 and those found can be crossed off the list as in Table 1.6. *Stop reading and continue solving the problem.*

5	1	4	6	0	3	3	5
6	5	4	6	2	2	4	0
4	5	4	5	0	0	2	5
6	2	1	3	3	6	3	0
4	2	3	5	0	1	6	6
0	1	4	1	4	1	5	6
2	1	3	2	0	3	2	1

Figure 1.4.

Table 1.6. First four dominoes checked off the list.

0̶0̶						
01	11					
02	12	22				
03	13	23	33			
04	14	24	34	4̶4̶		
05	15	25	35	4̶5̶	5̶5̶	
06	16	26	36	46	56	66

At this point we have identified enough dominoes by the process of trial and error to be able to discover others just by the geometry of the boundaries. In the upper left-hand corner 51 and 64 must be grouped together to avoid leaving a number isolated in such a way that it cannot be used to form a domino. Another way to use previous information is to remember that once a pair has been used it cannot be used again. That's where crossing pairs off the list helps. Because 64 has been used already, the 6 in the middle of the first column must be grouped with 2. Continuing in this manner the board looks like that shown in Figure 1-5, and our checklist is shown in Table 1.7. *Stop reading and complete the board if you have not already done so.*

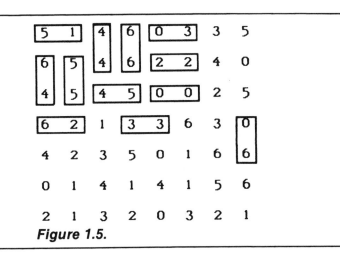

Figure 1.5.

Many pairs can now be found by checking to see if there is only one way to form them. The complete solution to the problem is shown in Figure 1.6.

Table 1.7. First twelve dominoes checked off the list.

~~00~~						
01	11					
02	12	~~22~~				
~~03~~	13	23	~~33~~			
04	14	24	34	~~44~~		
05	~~15~~	25	35	~~45~~	~~55~~	
~~06~~	16	~~26~~	36	~~46~~	56	~~66~~

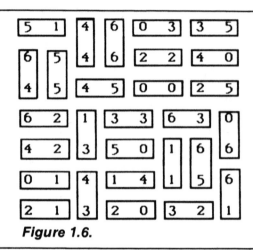

Figure 1.6.

STRATEGIES VS. RULES

My goal, as stated in the beginning of this chapter, is to teach general strategies that can be used in attacking any type of problem. This is in contrast to the rules or algorithms that one learns from a mathematical textbook for solving specific types of problems. For example, in elementary algebra you learn to translate specific types of story problems into algebraic equations using variables such as X and Y and then to apply special techniques to get a solution. As long as the problems can be solved in a similar way, everything is fine. But what do you do when you get stuck or the problem does not fit nicely into a category you know? This is one situation when the skills and strategies presented here and in later chapters become valuable.

As an example of such strategies, consider the game of checkers. The goal is to capture your opponent's pieces, and the operations are the legal moves. No one can give you a rule that will guarantee a win, but there are a number of good strategies that will improve your chances. Some of these strategies are (1) dominate the center of the board; (2) avoid getting your pieces too scattered out; (3) exchange pieces with your opponent only if it accomplishes some definite purpose; (4) a broken-up position with scattered pieces by your opponent should be attacked with full force; and (5) consolidate your own pieces as you move forward. The problem-solving strategies to be discussed in subsequent chapters are much like the winning strategies for checkers. They provide ways to systematically proceed in a variety of situations.

SUMMARY

As with most things in life, we are much more successful at solving problems when we are organized and take a systematic approach. It is usually helpful to analyze a problem in terms of three major components—the *givens*, the *goal*, and the *operations* (that can be performed in the domain of the problem). This helps us consciously attend to details that might otherwise be overlooked and to recognize assumptions and interpretations that we make.

Although there are differences among people, all of us have limited memory capacity, especially in the short term. Thus, it is useful to do whatever we can to compensate for that limit. One technique is to choose some appropriate symbols to represent the basic elements in the problem. Furthermore, it is important to find a good method to organize the information we generate from the analysis of the problem and the additional information that we generate as we attempt to solve it. Some type of chart or graph is usually very helpful for this purpose.

Practice Problems

TUG-OF-WAR

Susan, Marie, Karen, and Angie were amusing themselves one day by playing tug-of-war. Although it was hard, Marie could just outpull Susan and Karen together. Marie and Susan together could just hold Angie and Karen, neither pair being able to budge the other. However, if Karen and Susan changed places, then Angie and Susan won rather easily. Of the four girls, who was the strongest, next strongest, and so on?

THE DAIRY FARM

Four black cows and three brown cows give as much milk in five days as three black cows and five brown cows give in four days. Which kind of cow is the better milker, black or brown?

TRAINS

If it takes twice as long for a passenger train to pass a freight train after it first overtakes it as it takes the two trains to pass when going in opposite directions, how many times faster than the freight train is the passenger train?

REVERSE

The object is to rearrange the list of digits 4231 so they appear in numerical order 1234. Each move consists of reversing either two, three, or four of the digits all in a string beginning from the left. For example, starting with 4231, if you reverse the first three digits, the result is 3241. The object is to get from 4321 to 1234 in only four reverses.

THREE MOVES

Place three piles of matches on a table, one with eleven matches, the second with seven, and the third with six. You are to move the matches so that each pile holds eight matches. You may add to any pile only as many matches as it already contains, and all the matches must come from one other pile. For example, if a pile holds six matches, you may add six to it, no more or less. You have three moves.

COUNTING SQUARES

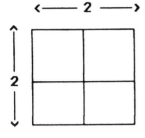

How many squares do you see? Four? Five? There are four 1-unit squares and one 2-unit squares for a total of five.

2 by 2 square

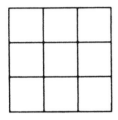

3 by 3 square

How many squares do you see?

Number of 1-unit squares _____

Number of 2-unit squares _____

Number of 3-unit squares _____

Total _____

On another piece of paper, draw a 4 by 4 and a 5 by 5 square. Count the squares, record your results in some kind of table, and list the number of each n-unit squares up to the highest possible unit value. Without drawing a 6 by 6 array, how many squares of each unit size would you expect to find?

TWENTY

There are three ways to add four odd numbers and get 10:

$$1 + 1 + 3 + 5 = 10 \qquad 1 + 1 + 1 + 7 = 10 \qquad 1 + 3 + 3 + 3 = 10$$

Changes in the order of numbers do not count as new solutions. Now add eight odd numbers to get twenty. To find all eleven solutions you will need to be systematic.

BELL HOP

Three persons arrive at the Nelson Hotel and pay $30 for their room together. Later, the manager discovers that she has overcharged them and dispatches the bellhop to give back $5. On the way the bellhop decides to take his own tip (to make sure he gets one) and keeps $2 for himself, returning only $3 to the guests. Thus, each guest has paid only $9 for the room and the bellhop has kept $2. That makes a total of $27 + $2 = $29. What happened to the extra dollar?

CHANGE

How many ways can you make change for a quarter using any combination of pennies, nickels, or dimes?

TRIANGLES

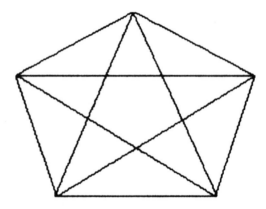

How many triangles are there in the figure?

LOCK YOUR LOCKERS

At Gauss High School there are fifty students and fifty lockers (numbered 1-50). At the beginning all the lockers were closed, then the first student came by and opened every locker. Following the first student, the second student came along and closed every second locker. The third student came along and reversed the condition of every third locker (if it was open he closed it, if it was closed he opened it). The fourth student reversed the condition of every fourth locker, etc. Finally, the fiftieth student reversed the condition of the fiftieth locker (the last one). Now, which lockers are open?

SILVER DOLLARS

Bob has ten pockets in his coat and forty-four silver dollars. He wants to put his silver dollars into his pockets distributed such that each pocket contains a different number of dollars. Can he do it?

Inference

In addition to symbolizing, organizing, and finding useful representations for information, one of the most basic strategies of problem solving is that of inference. Basically, *inference* is another term for logical reasoning. Although a basic course in logic is certainly beyond the scope of this book, we discuss some of the basic components of inference and then show how they are used in solving problems. Most of us possess basic logical skills, or we wouldn't be able to solve the many problems that we face every day. Interestingly enough, however, we don't always apply the skills as systematically and consistently as we should. Logical reasoning is useful because it allows us to establish new information (conclusions) from related information we already know. In this way, information in a problem can be connected in a logical chain until we finally arrive at a solution. Generally, logical reasoning can be broadly classified as either deductive or inductive. One of the major differences between the two is that with deduction we can be certain of a conclusion (even though it may not always be true), whereas with induction we can have only varying degrees of confidence in a necessarily uncertain conclusion. We'll now discuss some of the other differences between the two as they apply to practical situations.

DEDUCTION

In the simplest form of deductive reasoning, we start with at least two related statements or facts (called premises) from which we can draw a conclusion. If both statements are true the conclusion must also be true, if our logic is sound. For example, assume the following two statements are true: (1) All politicians are dishonest; (2) all dishonest people are liars. From these statements we can deduce with certainty that all politicians are liars, and this adds to our knowledge. There are several types of logical errors that people make, such as concluding from the above information that all liars are politicians. Also, people sometimes make erroneous conclusions, not because of errors in logic, but because they have certain biases that inappropriately influence their thinking. For example, the conclusion that all politicians are liars may not be true because one of the premises (all politicians are dishonest?) may not be true.

When it comes to problem solving, probably the greatest difficulty for most people in terms of logical reasoning is the failure to attempt the necessary inferences in the first place. One reason for this is that frequently all the necessary information for solving a problem is not stated explicitly; it is assumed to be part of common knowledge or is a common characteristic of an object discussed in the problem. Therefore, some of the necessary inferences are based on statements that are implicit or "hidden."

For example, assume you are preparing to leave on a picnic. A friend might tell you only that it is beginning to rain and then expect you to use that statement along with an implicit one from your own experience (rain makes you wet and uncomfortable) to conclude that you should reconsider your plans. In solving problems, therefore, it is always a good idea to review the givens and to note any implicit information that seems remotely relevant. Frequently, it turns out to be very relevant.

INDUCTION

Before getting involved in actually solving a problem with the strategy of inference, let us talk briefly about the other form of reasoning: induction. As mentioned earlier, induction differs from deduction in that conclusions are never certain. This is because induction depends on a set of specific experiences from which a consistent pattern may be inferred. Our conclusions, therefore, take the form of a general statement or rule that applies to all or most objects like those we have observed. For example, suppose you are acquainted with four people who have red hair and freckles. Such a state of affairs might lead you to conclude (inductively) that all red-headed people have freckles and vice versa. Your confidence in that induction would be directly related to the number of observations consistent with it. Thus, if you are told that Pamela Johnson has red hair, you will likely conclude (based on your observations that red-headed people have freckles) that she also has freckles. You can't be absolutely certain of your conclusion, however, because Pamela might just be different from all the red-headed people you've met previously. Now let us see how inference is used in solving problems.

GIVENS

As indicated in Chapter 1, the first place to start in analyzing a problem is with the *givens*. In fact, some problems can almost be solved by doing only that. As an example, *stop reading and try to solve the Tennis Pro's Problem in Figure 2.1.*

Figure 2.1. Tennis Pro's Problem.

Three tennis pros—Larry, Arthur, and Don—are counting up their money for the year. Arthur is a bachelor. The oldest of the three has a daughter learning to play. Larry earns the least money but is not the youngest. The largest income is earned by the oldest. List the pros in order of increasing age.

From the first statement, "Arthur is a bachelor," and our observations that most bachelors have no children (induction), we can infer that Arthur most likely has no children. From the second statement, "The oldest of the three has a daughter learning to play," and our observation that most people with children are married (another induction), we can infer that the oldest is probably married. It may seem a waste of time at this point to draw all of these inferences, because some of them may be irrelevant. However, experience has shown that it is better to discard irrelevant information later than to miss some information that is critical to the solution of the problem.

Before we continue with the problem, we need to determine a method for representing and organizing information in the problem. In this case, the goal gives a clue. Because any of the three players could be ranked in any of three positions according to age, we could use a table such as that shown in Table 2.1. We simply list all possibilities and see if some can either be confirmed or eliminated using the information contained in the problem. This also provides a useful way to keep track of new information we derive while working on the problem.

Table 2.1. Beginning table for the Tennis Pros Problem.

	YOUNGEST	MIDDLE	OLDEST
Arthur	?	?	?
Larry	?	?	?
Don	?	?	?

Earlier we inferred from the first statement that Arthur has no children. From this and the second statement we can deduce that Arthur must not be the oldest; from the third statement we find that Larry is not the youngest. Let us enter this information in the table, so that we do not forget it (see Table 2.2).

Table 2.2. Tennis Pros Problem partially solved.

	YOUNGEST	MIDDLE	OLDEST
Arthur	?	?	No
Larry	No	?	?
Don	?	?	?

At first, you might question the value of keeping track of what people are not in addition to what they are. However, as you will see, it is often possible to show that information contradicts all but one of the alternatives. Then, logically, that one remaining alternative must be the correct one, even though we could not prove that directly.

For example, as we compare the third and fourth statements, we can infer that Larry is not the oldest because he doesn't earn the most money, which the oldest does. If Larry isn't the youngest, and he isn't the oldest, then we may infer that he must be in the middle, because that is the only remaining possibility. Furthermore, if Larry is in the middle, then we can also infer that neither Arthur nor Don can be in the middle. It is time to update our table (see Table 2.3). You should now be able to see the value of this type of chart in making all the information easily available for use in further work with the problem.

Table 2.3. Tennis Pros Problem almost solved.

	YOUNGEST	MIDDLE	OLDEST
Arthur	?	No	No
Larry	No	Yes	No
Don	?	No	?

Analyzing the information in our table further, we see that Arthur is neither in the middle nor is the oldest. Therefore, he must be the youngest, so we can also infer that Don is not the youngest. If Don is not the youngest and he is not the middle (because Larry is), we can infer that he must be the oldest. This illustrates the value of having a useful representation for the problem in order to keep the information organized in a way that we can make good use of it in further work on the problem. Thus, we have solved the problem by continuing to make inferences from the givens, updating our information, and attempting to make additional inferences. In the Tennis Pros Problem, drawing inferences from the givens was sufficient to derive a solution. Let us examine a more difficult example requiring a similar procedure. It is found in Figure 2.2. *Stop reading and try to solve it!*

Figure 2.2. Banking Partners Problem.

The manager, the accountant, the teller, and the auditor at our bank are Ms. Green, Ms. White, Mr. Black, and Mr. Brown, but I can never tell who does what. (1) Mr. Brown is taller than the auditor or the teller; (2) The manager lunches alone; (3) Ms. White plays cards with Mr. Black; (4) The tallest of the four plays basketball; (5) Ms. Green lunches with the auditor and the teller; (6) Mr. Black is older than the auditor; (7) Mr. Brown plays no sports. Can you help me determine, for certain, just who does what?

As before, let us begin by drawing all additional inferences from the givens that are possible. This time we will number them continuing on from the seven statements listed in the problem. From the first statement and our commonsense knowledge that people can't be taller than themselves, we can infer:

8. Brown is not the auditor or the teller.

Similarly, from the fifth statement we can infer:

9. Green is not the auditor or the teller.

From statements two and five we can infer:

10.   Green also is not the manager.

From statement six we can infer:

11.   Black is not the auditor.

From the fourth and the seventh statements we can infer:

12.   Brown is not the tallest of the three.

Before proceeding with additional inferences, it is necessary to find a way to keep track of the information directly related to the solution. As with the Tennis Pros Problem, a table listing the names down the side and the occupations across the top is helpful. An example showing the information derived thus far is shown in Table 2.4.

Table 2.4. Representation for the Banking Partners Problem.

	MANAGER	ACCOUNTANT	TELLER	AUDITOR
Black	?	?	?	No
Brown	?	?	No	No
White	?	?	?	?
Green	No	?	No	No

From the information in the table, we can now infer that White (and no one else) is the auditor and that Green (and no one else) is the accountant. This information (with additional implied negatives) is shown in Table 2.5.

Table 2.5. Partial solution to the Banking Partners Problem.

	MANAGER	ACCOUNTANT	TELLER	AUDITOR
Black	?	No	?	No
Brown	?	No	No	No
White	No	No	No	Yes
Green	No	Yes	No	No

By analyzing the information in the table once more, we can infer that Black is the teller and Brown is the manager, which solves the problem. This problem is another good example of the importance of keeping track of the information so it can be used most effectively in making valid inferences.

GOALS

The Tennis Pros and the Banking Partners Problems illustrate the value of drawing additional inferences from the givens. To illustrate the importance of drawing inferences from goals as the primary means of solving a problem, consider the Portrait Paid in Gold Problem in Figure 2.3. *Stop reading the text and try to solve the problem.*

Figure 2.3. Portrait Paid in Gold Problem.

Many years ago, before there was an official coinage system, a wealthy countess kept her money in bars of gold that were 15 centimeters long each. One day she contracted with an artist to paint her portrait for her husband's birthday. The artist said that the portrait would take fifteen days to complete and that he wished to be paid 1 centimeter of gold each day. The countess agreed, but when she went to her local goldsmith, she was told that the gold cutters were very busy and they would have time to make only three cuts on her bar of gold in the next fifteen days. After some careful thought, the countess found a way to meet the artist's demands by cutting the bar into only four pieces. How did she do it?

In analyzing the givens, not much can be inferred beyond what is given. In analyzing the goal, it seems clear that the artist needs to be paid at the rate of 1 centimeter of gold per day, with the restriction that the task must be accomplished by cutting the 15-centimeter bar into only four pieces. The difficulty comes in determining what operations are possible, given the particular goal. When you read the statement "He wished to be paid 1 centimeter of gold each day" you probably inferred that the only possible operation was to literally give the artist 1 centimeter of gold per day. However, because this requires that the bar be cut into fifteen pieces, obviously it is not an acceptable solution. *Stop reading and try again to solve the problem.*

Actually, the artist needs only to have in his possession 1 centimeter of gold more each day than he had on the previous day; he doesn't literally need to be given a 1-centimeter piece of gold each day. If you can answer the following question, you should be able to make the necessary inference to solve the problem. How could you give someone $.50 if you only had a dollar bill? The answer to this question should lead you to infer that the countess must have cut her bar into pieces such that she could make change with the artist each day, leaving the artist with one more centimeter of gold than he had on the previous day. *Stop reading and try to solve the problem if you have not done so already!*

The operations now consist of finding the smallest pieces that will allow the countess to make change to accomplish the goal with no more than four pieces. Before proceeding with the solution, we now need to find a way to represent the information. For this purpose, a table would be useful listing the days, the pieces given to the artist by the countess, and the pieces in possession of the artist. A table giving all the information generated is shown in Table 2.6 on page 30.

OPERATIONS

Thus far we have discussed the importance of drawing inferences from the givens and goals. We now turn to a discussion of solving problems primarily by drawing important inferences regarding the operations to be performed. Consider the Gold Necklace Problem in Figure 2.4. *Stop reading and try to solve it*, paying particular attention to drawing inferences about the operations. Following the usual order, first analyze the givens.

Table 2.6. Solution to the Portrait Paid in Gold Problem.

DAYS	PIECES GIVEN ARTIST	PIECES TAKEN BACK	PIECES WITH ARTIST
1	1		1
2	2	1	2
3	1		2, 1
4	4	2, 1	4
5	1		4, 1
6	2	1	4, 2
7	1		4, 2, 1
8	8	4, 2, 1	8
9	1		8, 1
10	2	1	8, 2
11	1		8, 2, 1
12	4	2, 1	8, 4
13	1		8, 4, 1
14	2	1	8, 4, 2
15	1		8, 4, 2, 1

Figure 2.4. Gold Necklace Problem.

A young girl was given four separate pieces of gold chain that are each three links in length. The links are closed. She would like to have a necklace made for her mother with all twelve links in a closed loop. She is told by the jeweler that it costs $.02 to open a link and $.03 to close a link. The girl has only $.15 to pay the jeweler. How can she have the necklace made for that price?

The given information is quite simple, and the only inference that even seems remotely relevant is that the price of opening and closing a link is $.05. The goal is also quite clear. We start with four pieces of chain and want to make one continuous piece. We are given that it costs $.02 to open a link and $.03 to close a link, and there is only $.15 to pay for the job.

As indicated earlier, there is a very important inference regarding the way the operations are performed that is the key to the solution of the problem. *Stop reading and try to solve the problem if you have not already done so.*

You may have been stumped because you tried to join the four pieces of chain at their ends. Any way you try to do it, this results in opening and closing four links (one for each length), and that costs $.20. To spend only $.15 means you must find a way to join the chains by opening and closing only three links. Given that simple inference, look carefully at the givens one more time. *Stop reading and try to solve the problem if you have not already done so.*

The critical idea is that you can open all the links of one piece and use them to join the remaining three pieces. The best way to represent information in this problem probably is to draw pictures or diagrams showing the various pieces of chain.

Now we turn to a more involved problem that requires the use of inferences about operations. It is located in Figure 2.5 on page 32. *Stop reading and try to solve it.*

First, we should make explicit the properties of a beam balance, noting that the balance consists of a beam holding two pans that exactly balance each other. Therefore, two things are equal in weight when they cause the beam to be exactly level. When the beam doesn't balance, the heavier item causes its pan to be lower than the other. The goal is simply to determine the heavy coin in a maximum of three weighings. The basic operations consist of using the balance to weigh sets of coins to determine the heavy one. The most useful way to represent the information in the problem is to draw pictures and/or use a chart or table indicating the various weighing combinations and the number of coins eliminated from consideration.

The most obvious application of the operations does not solve the problem in three weighings. You might begin by dividing the coins into two piles of twelve, then divide the heavy pile from that weighing (it must contain the heavy coin) into two piles of six, divide the heavy pile from that weighing into piles of three, and use one or more weighings to determine which of the three remaining coins is the heavy one. This procedure does not solve the problem, but it

Figure 2.5. Gold Coin Problem.

Tom's uncle offered to give him a gold coin if Tom could pick it out from among twenty-three *other* coins that looked just like it but were made from a copper and brass alloy. Because gold is heavier than copper and brass, Tom's uncle was willing to let Tom use a beam balance for weighing the coins to aid him in his choice. However, Tom was allowed to make only three weighings. How did he do it?

does provide a hint to the correct procedure. The critical inference to solve the problem in three weighings lies in the way the balance is used to determine which of the final three coins is the heavy one. It can be done in only one weighing by placing any two coins in the balance. If the beam doesn't balance you can readily identify the heavy coin; but if it does balance then the remaining coin is the heavy one. Thus, two-thirds of the remaining coins can be eliminated from consideration in only one weighing, whereas previously the balance was used to eliminate only half of the remaining coins with each weighing. *Stop reading and try to solve the problem if you have not already done so.*

The balance can be used to eliminate two-thirds of the remaining coins from consideration on each weighing by dividing them into three, rather than two equal piles. Even when one of the three piles has an extra coin, two of them can still be eliminated by weighing the two equal piles to see if they balance. A table for keeping track of information is shown in Table 2.7.

Table 2.7. Solution to the Gold Coin Problem.

WEIGHING	COINS IN EACH PILE	COINS REMAINING
1	8	8
2	2 or 3	2 or 3
3	1	1

MENTAL SET

In many of the problems discussed in this chapter we found that difficulties can arise not only from failing to draw an appropriate inference, but because we may have drawn an inappropriate one. Often this happens because the problem information is stated in a way that causes us to draw an inference that is opposite to (or at least different from) the correct one, and therefore actually interferes with our drawing the correct one. This situation has been labeled by psychologists as an inappropriate "mental set," which means merely that people get so locked into thinking about a problem in a particular way that they can't think about it in a way that will lead to a solution. A good example is illustrated in the following problem:

Two people boarded a bus in Chicago. One person was the father of the other person's son. How could this be?

Stop reading and try to solve the problem.

If you had difficulty with this problem, it is probably because you inferred that both persons were males because the information in the problem described only males. What other inferences about the sex of the two people could be made? The correct inference is that one person is female. If one person is the father of the other person's son, the other person could be only the mother. Let us consider another example of mental set, or incorrect inference, in the following problem:

As he was passing through O'Hare International Airport one day, Mr. Henry Benson met a friend whom he had not seen in years. Beside his friend was a little girl. "Henry!" shouted the friend. "How good to see you after all these years. Did you know that I have married? This is my daughter." "Hello," said Benson to the little girl. "What is your name?" "It's the same as my mother's," replied the girl. "Then you must be Susan," said Benson. How did he know her name?

Stop reading and try to solve the problem.

You probably had an easier time with this problem, but if you had difficulty, it was probably because you inferred (incorrectly) that the friend was male because Henry was male. Once you entertain the notion that Henry's friend could be female, the solution to the problem is trivial. There is no easy way to instruct someone how to avoid becoming the victim of incorrect mental sets. However, becoming aware of their potential hazards should help. There are a couple of things you can do to help overcome their effects. Carefully analyze the givens, and try to consciously recognize any assumptions about the problem information that you are making automatically. Then if you get stumped, go back and critically evaluate each of them. You will often find that there are alternative interpretations or inferences that could be made. By systematically trying all of them, you will be more likely to avoid getting caught by an inappropriate mental set.

SUMMARY

In addition to symbolizing, organizing, and finding useful representations for problems, a fundamental aspect of analyzing and solving problems are the many inferences we draw. These inferences basically take one of two forms, deduction and induction. Deductive conclusions stem from at least two statements (called premises) that we accept as true, and therefore a conclusion necessarily follows. The conclusion may be incorrect either because our logic is faulty or because one or more of the premises is false. On the other hand, inductive conclusions are generalizations or rules we derive from a set of specific observations. Because the rules we form are a function of only the particular set of experiences we have had, inductive conclusions are necessarily uncertain. With regard to both types of inferences, the greatest difficulty people have in solving problems is in their failure to carefully evaluate the information before drawing any inferences.

Many times we have difficulty in drawing the appropriate inferences because we automatically are led into an inappropriate one as a result of the way in which the information in the problem is stated. In extreme forms this is called an inappropriate mental set. Although there is no certain way to avoid the perils of such mental sets, they can be overcome by attempting to be very conscious about the inferences we make and critically evaluating them to determine if there are alternatives within the context of the problem. Frequently we find that there are alternatives that are helpful in solving a particular problem.

Practice Problems

LINE COUNT

Using a ruler, draw as many lines as you can through pairs of points found in each lettered section. Count the number of lines and record this number in the place indicated.

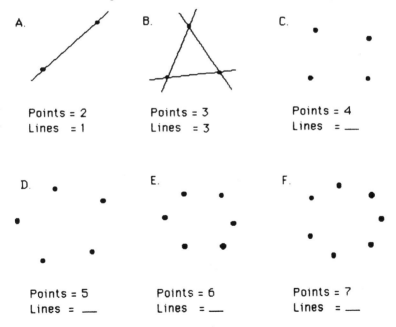

A.

Points = 2
Lines = 1

B.

Points = 3
Lines = 3

C.

Points = 4
Lines = ___

D.

Points = 5
Lines = ___

E.

Points = 6
Lines = ___

F.

Points = 7
Lines = ___

Without drawing the lines corresponding to eight or nine points, what would you expect the number of lines to be for each of them?

DIAGONAL COUNT

A diagonal of a polygon is a line connecting two nonconsecutive vertices. Draw all the diagonals you can from each vertex in the polygons below and record your results in the blanks.

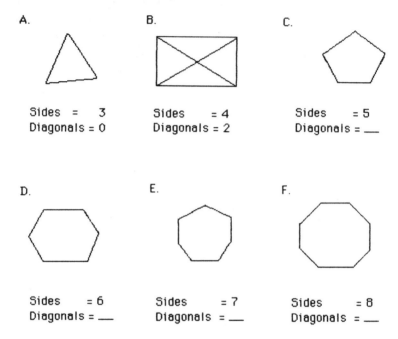

A.

Sides = 3
Diagonals = 0

B.

Sides = 4
Diagonals = 2

C.

Sides = 5
Diagonals = ___

D.

Sides = 6
Diagonals = ___

E.

Sides = 7
Diagonals = ___

F.

Sides = 8
Diagonals = ___

Without drawing the diagonals corresponding to a nine-sided polygon, what would you expect the number to be?

A BOTTLE'S VOLUME

You have a bottle, approximately two-thirds filled with liquid, that has a round, square, or rectangular bottom that is flat. It has a tapered neck and sides that are straight between the bottom of the bottle and the beginning of the neck. How can you find (calculate) the volume of the entire bottle using only a ruler for measurement? You may not add or pour out liquid. (Don't hesitate to get a bottle and work with it.)

COFFEE WITH YOUR MILK?

Two people enter a diner for a work break. One likes a little milk in her coffee, and the other likes a little coffee in his milk. One orders a cup of black coffee, and the other asks for a cup of milk. To satisfy their tastes, one teaspoon of milk is taken from the cup of milk and mixed with the cup of coffee. Then a teaspoon of the coffee-with-milk mixture is added to the milk. The question is: Is there more milk in the coffee, more coffee in the milk, or the same amount of coffee in the milk as there is milk in the coffee?

THE REASONING OF AGE

Jack and Stan are the same age. Jack is older than Bob, who in turn is older than Karen. Kent, although older than Karen, is younger than Jack and Bob. Stan is younger than Kent's friend Steve. List the six people according to their relative ages.

ARCHIMEDES AND HIS PET ROCK

Back in the days when pet rocks were in vogue, Archimedes took his pet rock on a trip across a lake. On route, Archimedes and the rock got into an argument that resulted in the rock being thrown overboard. The rock immediately sank to the bottom of the lake. The question is: Did the water level in the lake rise or fall? In order to answer the question you are given the following information from Archimedes' book *On Floating Bodies*: Any object that floats in water always has a certain portion submerged, which displaces some water. The amount of the water displaced is equal to the weight of the object. On the other hand, if the object sinks, the amount of the water displaced is less than the weight of the object.

THE TENNIS PLAYER

Two women, Alice and Carol, and two men, Brian and David, are athletes. One is a swimmer, a second is a skater, a third is a gymnast, and a fourth is a tennis player. One day they were seated around a square table, one per side as follows:

1.   The swimmer sat on Alice's left.
2.   The gymnast sat across from Brian.
3.   Carol and David sat next to each other.
4.   A woman sat on the skater's left.

Who is the tennis player?

A PIECE OF CAKE

Mrs. Miller decided to make cakes for a bake sale. Each white cake she made required two cups of flour and one cup of sugar. Each German chocolate cake required the same amount of flour but twice as much sugar. When she was finished, Mrs. Miller had used ten cups of flour and seven cups of sugar. How many white cakes did she make?

GAUSS

A story is told of Gauss, the famous mathematician, when he was a child in school. His teacher gave the class an assignment to find the sum of the numbers from 1 to 100. The purpose of the task was mainly to keep them busy for a considerable period of time. Much to the teacher's dismay, Gauss had the answer in just a moment or two. He had accomplished the task by observing in the set of numbers some interesting patterns that suggested a shortcut to just adding all the numbers in succession. Can you discover his method?

TWO TRAINS

A nonstop train leaves New York for Washington traveling at a constant speed of 60 miles per hour. At the same time, another nonstop train leaves Washington for New York traveling at an average speed of 40 miles per hour. How far apart are the trains, one hour before they pass each other?

THE WOODSMAN

A woodsman paddling steadily across the still surface of a northern lake saw a magnificent bass break water directly ahead of him. Twelve strokes he counted until his canoe first crossed the ever-widening circle of ripples the fish had made, and then twelve more strokes before he broke through the ripples on the opposite side of the circle. For a time thereafter he sought relief from the pleasant monotony of his journey by calculating how far from him (how many strokes) the fish had been at the moment it jumped, but it proved too much for him. Can you solve the problem?

COW, GOAT, AND GOOSE

A farmer has a pasture that he must use to best advantage to feed his livestock, which consists of a cow, a goat, and a goose. He has found that the goat and the goose eat just as much grass as the cow and that the pasture will last in either case just ninety days. Furthermore, he has found that the field will pasture the cow and the goose for sixty days; or it will pasture the cow and the goat for forty-five days. He would now like to know how long the field would pasture all three animals without first trying it, because if it did not last long enough he might not be able to find additional pasture when needed.

CHANGE PARTNERS

Four married couples, consisting of Alice, Betty, Carol, Dorothy, Ed, Frank, Harry, and George, went to the country club dance one Saturday evening not long ago. At one time as a result of exchanging dances, Betty was dancing with Ed, Alice was dancing with Carol's husband, Dorothy was dancing with Alice's husband, Frank was dancing with George's wife, and George was dancing with Ed's wife. Who is married to whom and who is dancing with whom?

Trial
and Error

One of the easiest methods for solving problems is the method of trial and error. This method consists of (1) choosing an acceptable operation, (2) performing the operation on the givens, and (3) testing to see if the goal has been reached. If the answer to (3) is no, the process is repeated until the goal is reached or it becomes obvious that the problem is impossible to solve. Because it is one of the easiest methods to use, trial and error is sometimes looked upon as the lazy person's method or the method to use when you aren't smart enough to do anything else. However, this criticism is usually intended for a special case, which we shall call *random trial and error*. The intent of this chapter is to teach you that some other forms of trial and error can be quite powerful and effective as methods of problem solving. To begin, consider the Pigs and Chickens Problem presented in Figure 3.1 on page 44. *Stop reading and try to solve it.*

As discussed in Chapter 1, the first thing you should do in attacking this problem is to determine the givens, the goal, and the operations that can be performed on the givens. In this case, the givens are: (1) a total of eighteen animals, (2) a total of fifty legs, and (3) each pig has four legs, whereas each chicken has only two. This last bit of information is not stated in the problem, of course, but can be inferred from our knowledge of chickens and pigs. (Recall that in Chapter 2, we discussed ways of inferring additional information from givens as a basic problem-solving strategy.) The goal is to determine how many chickens and how many pigs there are. The operations are simply arithmetic operations of addition and multiplication used to compute the numbers of animals and

Figure 3.1. Pigs and Chickens Problem.

Judy and Ted went to visit their grandfather's farm. While there, they saw a pen of pigs and chickens. Ted said he had counted eighteen animals altogether; Judy said she counted a total of fifty legs. How many pigs were there?

legs. Any solution to this problem must satisfy two conditions: (1) The number of chickens plus the number of pigs must equal eighteen and (2) the number of chicken legs plus the number of pig legs must equal fifty. Those whose algebra skills are current will recognize this as a problem which could be solved with "two equations and two unknowns." However, our interest is in how it could be solved using various means of trial and error. As suggested in Chapter 1, we begin by choosing a way to represent or symbolize the information in the problem so that we don't have to rely on our memories to keep track of it. One way is a simple table with a column for the number of chickens, the number of pigs, and the total number of legs as shown in Table 3.1. *Stop reading and try to solve this problem if you have not done so already.*

Table 3.1. Representation for the Pigs and Chickens Problem.

PIGS	CHICKENS	LEGS
18	0	72 too many legs
0	18	36 too few legs

RANDOM TRIAL AND ERROR

As mentioned earlier, one type of trial and error is called random trial and error. Applying this strategy, we haphazardly choose a number less than or equal to eighteen for the number of pigs, subtract it from eighteen for the number of chickens and compute the number of legs. If the total isn't fifty, we haphazardly choose another number for the pigs and repeat the process. A sample solution is shown in Table 3.2.

Table 3.2. Solution to the Pigs and Chickens Problem using random trial and error.

PIGS	CHICKENS	LEGS
3	15	42
10	8	56
16	2	68
12	6	60
5	13	46
2	16	70
13	5	62
14	4	64
7	11	50 Solved!!!

As you can see, the method of haphazardly choosing a number for pigs may take a long time and therefore is not very efficient. This is especially true if we do not avoid repetitions of the same numbers. However, the method is easy to use and will eventually (by exhaustion) solve the problem.

SYSTEMATIC TRIAL AND ERROR

An improvement that would solve the problem more efficiently would be a system for choosing the numbers that is not haphazard.

This system should eliminate all duplications of trials and exhaust the possible solutions until one is found. *Stop reading and try to find a rule to systematically choose numbers for the Pigs and Chickens Problem.* We shall refer to this method as systematic trial and error.

One simple rule for this problem might be to start with zero pigs and eighteen chickens and continue to add a pig and subtract a chicken until the correct total of fifty legs is achieved. The information generated during the solution is listed in Table 3.3.

Table 3.3. Solution to the Pigs and Chickens Problem using systematic trial and error.

PIGS	CHICKENS	LEGS
0	18	36
1	17	38
2	16	40
3	15	42
4	14	44
5	13	46
6	12	48
7	11	50

Systematic trial and error may also generate many answers before the correct one is found, but it will always work (given an appropriate problem) and is more efficient and effective than random trial and error. However, it is desirable to be efficient as well as effective, so let's consider a further refinement of the trial-and-error method.

GUIDED TRIAL AND ERROR

In systematic trial and error we tested each answer only to see if it was the correct one or not. We could be more efficient by also testing each answer to see if it was closer or farther from the goal than the previous one. This information could then be used to guide our selection of numbers for the next trial. With this refinement, we have *guided trial and error.* If you did not solve the problem this way previously, *stop reading and try to do so.*

As with random trial and error we need a first trial, and we could choose it randomly or use the information in the givens to guide our first selection. Because each pig has twice as many legs as each chicken, we might try half as many pigs as chickens as a starting point (six pigs and twelve chickens). With six pigs and twelve chickens, the total number of legs is forty-eight, so we need to move in the direction of more pigs and fewer chickens. On the other hand, if we had begun with a combination giving more than fifty legs, we would need to move in the other direction of fewer pigs and more chickens. The table of values used to solve the problem this way is shown in Table 3.4. The result is a very efficient method of trial and error by (1) using a rule to systematically select the numbers, and (2) using the information from each trial to guide the selection of the values used for the next trial.

Table 3.4. Solution to the Pigs and Chickens
Problem using guided trial and error.

PIGS	CHICKENS	LEGS	NEXT TRIAL
6	12	48	add pigs
8	10	52	reduce pigs
7	11	50	solved

As mentioned earlier, the problem can be solved without trial and error by using elementary algebra. However, there is one drawback—people who have not used algebra for a few years often give up on solving a problem when they recognize that it could be done with algebra but know that they have forgotten how to use it. Algebra has been such a successful method for solving story problems in high school mathematics that people naturally assume that it is the only method. If you remember how to use algebra, you should not hesitate to do so, but you should also realize that many problems that you encounter, outside a mathematics text, can be solved without it. The Pigs and Chickens Problem is a good example.

Before we leave the Pigs and Chickens Problem, I would like to discuss one other interesting solution to it, one that uses a mental representation. Imagine that all the pigs are standing on their hind legs. How many legs are now touching the ground? Because there are eighteen animals, there should be thirty-six legs on the ground. How many are not touching the ground? Obviously, there are fourteen not touching the ground because there are fifty legs in all. What kinds of legs are those not touching the ground? They are pigs' legs. How many pigs are there? If there are fourteen pigs' legs, there would have to be seven pigs. Most people find this an intriguing solution but wonder how they would ever come up with it. Actually, it is not as mysterious as it might seem when you consider that it is just a "tricky" way of starting with a guess of no pigs and eighteen chickens. This would result in fourteen too few legs, which would need to be provided by trading seven chickens for seven pigs.

As another example of guided trial and error, consider the Taxes in Taxes Problem in Figure 3.2. *Stop reading and try to solve the problem.*

Figure 3.2. Taxes in Taxes Problem.

Naturally, many people believe that rich people should pay more taxes than poor people, because the wealthier ones have more money. But sometimes this policy is carried to extremes. In one place, the tax rate is the same as the number of thousands of dollars a person earns. For example, if a person earns $6,000, then his tax rate is 6 percent of that. But if a person earns $92,000, then his taxes are a whopping 92 percent of that. What income between $1 and $100,000 would leave you the most money after taxes?

In analyzing the givens, it is assumed that the reader understands the meaning of percent and how to calculate it. The formula is to multiply a particular value by the percent value and move the decimal two places to the left. Thus 6 percent of $6,000 is $360 and 92 percent of $92,000 is $84,640. Our goal is simply to find the income level that would yield the most money after taxes. The operations to be performed are (1) calculating taxes on various income levels, and (2) determining net income by subtracting taxes from gross income. In the case of the two numbers given in the problem, we find that the large income yields a net of $7,360, whereas the smaller one yields a net of $5,640. Thus, more would be realized from a gross income of $92,000 even though the tax rate is so much higher.

To use guided trial and error in solving the problem, the operations are (1) choose two values of gross income, (2) calculate the net on each, (3) compare the two, (4) take the gross yielding the larger net, and (5) choose a new gross, either smaller or larger, for comparison. This process is repeated until a gross is found that yields the highest net. As before, we also need a way to represent and keep track of information generated during the solution. A table for this purpose showing the gross and net incomes is shown in Table 3.5.

Table 3.5. Solution to the Taxes in Taxes Problem.

GROSS	NET	CONCLUSION	COMMENT
$ 6,000	$ 5,640	Choose >$6,000	For a comparison
92,000	7,360	Choose >92,000	Net getting larger
95,000	4,750	Choose <92,000	Net getting smaller
80,000	16,000	Choose <80,000	Net getting larger
65,000	22,750	Choose <65,000	Net getting larger
50,000	25,000	Choose <50,000	Net getting larger
35,000	22,750	Choose between 50,000 and 65,000	Net smaller
55,000	24,750	Choose between 50,000 and 35,000	Net larger
45,000	24,750	Must be 50,000	Halfway between 55,000 and 45,000
50,000	25,000	Problem solved.	

The problem illustrates how to use the results of each trial to guide the choice of values for the next one in order to get nearer the goal.

As a third example of guided trial and error, consider another tax problem, which is presented in Figure 3.3. *Stop reading and try to solve the problem.*

Figure 3.3. Johnny's Income Tax Problem.

"Mr. Thompson, will you help me figure my income tax?" asked Johnny, the office boy. "Sure thing," was the reply; "bring me your papers." "Well, here's the form I gotta use, and here's the statement of how much the company paid me during the year." "Any income from other sources? On the side?" "Naw, that's the whole thing." "Do you claim any deductions? Any capital losses? Any contributions to charity?" "I gave four bucks to the Red Cross." "And you have a receipt for it, don't you? Okay, you can claim that as a deduction. I don't suppose you are married, are you? Any dependents? No? Well, then, your personal exemption is $500. Your tax is 19 percent of the taxable net income. I'll work it out for you . . . here it is." "Gee," remarked Johnny. "Isn't that funny! The tax is just 10 percent of what the company paid me. Does it always work out that way?" "No, indeed," laughed Mr. Thompson. "That's just a happenstance." What was the amount of Johnny's tax?

In analyzing the givens we can infer that the net taxable income is the gross income from the company minus $504 ($500 for personal exemption and the $4 contribution to the Red Cross). Furthermore, we find that the tax is equal to both 10 percent of the gross and 19 percent of the net taxable income. The goal is to determine the tax, given these two conditions. The operations to be performed consist of (1) choosing values of the gross income, (2) calculating net income, and (3) calculating the tax as 10 percent of the gross and 19 percent of the net. The goal is reached when the two methods of calculating the tax yield identical results.

In order to use guided trial and error, it is necessary to choose values that lead closer and closer to the goal. In this problem, it is helpful to recognize that because the deductions are fixed, the higher the gross income, the higher percentage of gross the net will be. Also, because the tax rate is higher on the net, the amount of tax on the net will change more than the amount of tax on the gross as gross income changes. Therefore, when the tax based on the gross is higher than that based on the net, a higher gross will need to be chosen to reduce the relative difference between the two. On the other hand, when the tax based on gross income is lower, the value for the gross would need to be lowered.

In order to keep track of the information, it is useful to make a table listing the gross and net incomes and the taxes based on each. The information used to solve the problem is shown in Table 3.6.

Table 3.6. Solution to Johnny's Income Tax Problem.

GROSS INCOME	NET INCOME	TAX ON NET	TAX ON GROSS	DIFFERENCE (NET-GROSS)	DECISION
$2000	$1496	$284.24	$200.00	84.24	Choose lower gross
1500	996	189.24	150.00	39.24	Choose lower gross
1000	496	94.24	100.00	-5.76	Choose higher gross
1200	696	132.24	120.00	12.24	Choose lower gross
1050	546	103.74	105.00	-1.26	Choose higher gross
1060	556	105.64	106.00	- .36	Choose higher gross
1062	558	106.02	106.20	- .18	Choose higher gross
1064	560	106.40	106.40	-0.00	Problem solved

DETOUR PROBLEMS

In the three problems discussed in this chapter, we have stressed the importance of evaluating the information generated on each trial to determine whether or not it is closer or further from the goal than that generated on the previous trial. This evaluation can then be used to make a wiser choice on the following trial. However, once in a while we find a problem in which values or operations must be chosen that temporarily take us farther from the goal (or at least lead us no closer), but must be used in order to reach the goal. Such problems are called detour problems. An example of a detour problem is the Missionaries and Cannibals Problem in Figure 3.4. *Stop reading and try to solve it.*

Figure 3.4. *Missionaries and Cannibals Problem.*

Three missionaries and three cannibals arrive at a river bank in the middle of a thick jungle. They find a boat that holds only two people. The missionaries realize that they must be careful not to ever allow the cannibals to outnumber them, or they will risk being eaten. How can everyone get across the river without the cannibals having one of the missionaries for lunch?

Analysis of the givens and the goal indicates there isn't any information that is not stated explicitly. The operations are straightforward; in transferring one or two people across the river the missionaries must never outnumber the cannibals on either side.

One way to represent information in this problem is to draw a line on a piece of paper to represent the river and then to choose M and C to represent the missionaries and the cannibals, respectively. The symbols can then be moved across the line as you try to solve the problem. A new diagram will be used to represent the state of affairs after each one-way trip across the river. The entire solution is shown in Figure 3.5.

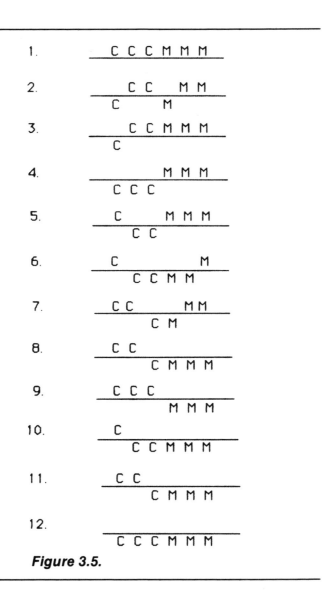

Figure 3.5.

For every trip there are three options for taking people across: (1) two cannibals, (2) two missionaries, or (3) one of each. The first consideration is that each trip must be made so that neither it nor the one following it will leave the missionaries outnumbered on either side of the river. Also, each round trip should result in one more person being on the goal side of the river than before. For example, for the first trip, it would be possible to send two cannibals across and have one bring the boat back. However, there would be no option open for the next trip that would not leave the missionaries outnumbered on one side or the other. Thus, it is necessary to send one cannibal and one missionary across on the first trip and have the missionary bring the boat back.

The difficult part of solving this problem for most people lies in steps 6 and 7 of Figure 3.5. Until then, each round trip results in getting closer to the goal. At that point, however, it is necessary to detour and make a round trip (steps 6 and 7) that leaves the number of people on the goal side unchanged. This step is necessary in order to proceed through the remainder of the solution without having the missionaries outnumbered at some point. Thus, sometimes when using guided trial and error, it may be necessary to execute a trial that does not directly bring one closer to the goal.

SUMMARY

The method of trial and error is often considered a relatively ineffective method for solving problems. Random trial and error probably deserves that reputation. However, there are variations of the method that can be very useful, especially guided trial and error. After analyzing the problem and establishing the relationships and conditions constraining the problem elements, you should pick values that are true for some of the conditions, test the remaining ones, and evaluate the outcome. In particular, you should compare the result with the goal to determine if you are closer to the goal. If so, do more of the same until you reach the goal. If not, you may need to "reverse directions," so to speak. By carefully evaluating your progress at each step, you will usually be able to solve the problem.

On rare occasions, you may find a problem that requires you to make a detour and do something that seems to be counterproductive, or at least nonproductive in the short term. Just be aware that these situations exist and be prepared to act accordingly when necessary.

Practice Problems

TEN FLOOR LAMPS

In a square living room, how do you place 10 floor lamps around the room so that there are an equal number of lamps along each wall?

MOVING CHECKERS

Move the checkers so that all the white ones end up on the left, followed by the black ones on the right, or vice versa (black on left and white on right). The checkers must be moved in pairs, taking adjacent checkers without disturbing their order and sliding them to a vacant place. Only three moves are necessary.

WEIGHING THE BABY

Mrs. O'Toole is a frugal person and is attempting to weigh herself, her baby, and her dog for only one dime at a dime-store pay scale. All of them weigh a total of 170 pounds. She weighs 100 pounds more than the baby and the dog together, and the dog weighs 60 percent less than the baby. How much does each weigh separately?

SETTLING THE BILL

After the boxing matches, a group of friends went into a restaurant for a midnight snack. "Put it all on one bill," they told the waiter. The bill amounted to $6, and the men agreed to split it equally. Then it was discovered that two of their number had slipped away without settling their scores, so that each of the remaining men was assessed $.25 more. How many men were in the party originally?

THE THREE BRIDES

A rich king announced that he would provide a dowry for his daughters in the amount of their weight in gold, so they were speedily suited by suitable suitors. All were married on the same day. Before weighing in, each partook of some exceedingly heavy wedding cake; of course, this all made the grooms very light-hearted. Collectively, the brides weighed 396 pounds. However, Nellie weighed 10 pounds more than Kitty, and Minnie weighed 10 pounds more than Nellie. One of the bridegrooms, John Brown, weighed just as much as his bride; William Jones weighed half again as much as his bride. Charles Robinson weighed twice as much as his bride. The brides and grooms together weighed half a ton. Which suitor was each daughter suited to?

TRADING CHICKENS

A farmer and his wife are at the market to trade their poultry for livestock on the basis of eighty-five chickens for a horse and a cow. In the current market, it is also true that five horses are worth twelve cows. The farmer and his wife have already chosen a minimum number of cows and horses, and now they are trying to decide whether to buy more horses or cows. The husband suggests that they should take as many more horses as they have purchased, and then they would only have seventeen horses and cows to feed through the winter. However, the wife points out that if they were to double the number of cows instead, they would then have only nineteen cows and horses to feed during the winter, it would require exactly the number of chickens they brought, and they would not have to take any back home. How many chickens did they take to the market with them?

SHARING APPLES

A gang of boys made a raid on the Perkins orchard and came back with a quantity of apples, which were then pooled and divided equally among them. Michael said he thought it would be fairer to share by families instead of individuals. As there were two Johnson brothers and two Fairbanks brothers, a redivision by families would have increased each share by three apples. With the argument at its height, along came Fred, who, being the oldest of the gang, was appealed to as arbiter. Fred decided that it would be unfair to share by families. Furthermore, he pointed out, he himself would certainly have participated in the raid, to the great increase of the booty, had he not been detained by a compulsory engagement with a rug-beater. But as head of the gang he was entitled to a share. Fred had a way of winning his arguments, so each boy contributed one apple to him, making equal shares all around. How many apples did the boys gather?

WOLF, GOAT, AND CABBAGE

A man has to take a wolf, a goat, and cabbage across a river. His rowboat has enough room for the man plus either the wolf or the goat or the cabbage. If he takes the wolf, the goat will eat the cabbage. If he takes the cabbage with him the wolf will eat the goat. Only when the man is present are the goat and the cabbage safe from their enemies. All the same, the man gets them all across the river. How?

Sub-goals

Most problems are solved in a series of steps that build on each other until the final goal is reached. The procedure of consciously and systematically dividing a problem into component parts and solving each part is referred to as the method of *sub-goals.* The power of the sub-goal strategy is illustrated in the following analogy: A bundle of sticks tied together may be impossible to break in half. However, if the bundle is untied and each stick is broken separately, the goal is easily attained. The same is true of most problems, especially complex ones. The strategy of sub-goals can be conceptualized as a three-step process:

1. Break the problem into sub-problems, keeping a record of the relations between these parts as part of the total problem.
2. Solve the sub-problems.
3. Combine the results to form a solution to the problem as a whole.

Many times there is a natural tendency to divide a problem into smaller components. However, the usefulness of sub-goals as a problem-solving method is fully realized only by consciously taking extra time and effort to divide a problem into component parts, each of which will be easier to solve than the problem as a whole. The problem in Figure 4.1 on page 62, Crossing the River, can be easily solved by using sub-goals. *Stop reading the text, read the problem, and try to solve it.*

The goal in this problem can be viewed as a series of sub-goals. Because it takes the same set of operations to get each man across the river, it is useful to define a sub-goal of getting one man across the river and both boys back on the side from which they started.

Figure 4.1. Crossing the River Problem.

Nine men and two boys want to cross a river, using a small canoe that will carry either one man or the two boys. How many times must the boat cross the river to accomplish this goal?

This set of operations could then be repeated nine times, once for each man. Finally, one last trip would be required to get the boys across. To organize the information in this problem, use a series of diagrams to represent the river and the positions of one man and the two boys after each crossing. The letters BBM stand for the positions of the two boys and a man. A new diagram is made to represent each move. *If you have not already solved it, stop reading and give the problem another try.*

Because the boat will not hold a man and a boy, it is important to get a boy across the river before sending a man across, or there will be no way to get the boat back across. Thus the sequence of crossings required to get one man across the river is as follows:

(1) Both boys cross the river in the boat; (2) one of the boys takes the boat back; (3) the man takes the boat across; and (4) the boy on that side takes the boat back to the starting point. This sequence of moves is illustrated in Figure 4.2.

Start	BBM	

1.	M	
	BB	

2.	BM	
	B	

3.	B	
	B M	

4.	BB	
	M	

Figure 4.2.

Because it requires four trips to transport one man across, thirty-six trips are required to get nine men across. Then one final trip will be required to get the boys across, making a total of thirty-seven trips. Thus, you can see that effective use of the method of sub-goals makes the solution considerably simpler than finding a solution by a method such as trial and error and then counting all the trips.

For another example of the use of sub-goals, *stop reading and try to solve the Farmer's Market Problem in Figure 4.3 on page 64.*

In analyzing the givens, we can infer from the second statement that if the farmer grossed $24 selling watermelons at $3 each, he must have sold eight melons in the morning. The rest of the information in the givens is explicit. Because the given information contains numbers, we can assume that the operations to be performed are arithmetic. The representation of information generated is a systematic listing of the result of each arithmetic operation so that it could be used in later stages of the solution.

In analyzing the goal, it is apparent that the gross sales for the entire day are a function of the morning gross and the afternoon gross. Because the morning gross is given, determination of the

Figure 4.3. Farmer's Market Problem.

A farmer took his watermelons to the market on Saturday. During the morning, he sold the melons for $3 each, grossing $24. During the afternoon, he reduced his price to $2 each and sold twice as many. What were his gross sales for the day?

afternoon gross becomes a useful sub-goal. The afternoon gross is, of course, the number of melons sold multiplied by the price per melon ($2). The problem states that the number sold in the afternoon is twice as many as were sold in the morning. Hence, the sub-goal of determining the afternoon gross can be broken further into sub-goals consisting of (1) determining the number sold in the morning, and (2) determining the number sold in the afternoon. As noted from the givens, the number of melons sold in the morning is eight ($24 ÷ $3 per melon). Thus, there must have been sixteen sold in the afternoon, resulting in a gross sales of $32 ($2 per melon × 16 melons). Adding the morning and afternoon sales yields a total of $56. This is a relatively easy problem, but it serves as a useful example to draw attention to the method of sub-goals.

For a more difficult example where this method can be used, consider the program in Figure 4.4. *Stop reading and try to solve it.*

Figure 4.4. Balance Problem.

How many glasses will balance a bottle?

After analyzing the given information, it should become apparent that the solution will require several steps, or sub-goals. If we spend a few moments actively searching for appropriate sub-goals, the solution can be obtained more easily. Figure 4.4 B shows that a bottle weighs as much as a glass plus a plate, so the problem could be solved by replacing the plate by its equivalent weight in glasses. Therefore, a useful sub-goal is to try to determine the number of glasses that will balance one plate. This relationship is not given explicitly in A, B, or C, so it is necessary to establish a second sub-goal. One possibility is to replace the two pitchers in balance C of Figure 4.4 with glasses and plates using the information in balances A and B of Figure 4.4. When this second sub-goal is achieved, it is possible to reduce the number of plates on

Figure 4.5.

both sides until the first sub-goal is achieved. From there, of course, the goal can be achieved. *Stop reading and try to solve the problem if you have not already done so.* The complete solution, represented in Figure 4.5, requires several additional steps, as we will now see.

As a rule, sub-goals are easier to attain than the entire goal, and this problem is no exception. Adding a glass to both sides of balance B in Figure 4.4 yields the balance D of Figure 4.5. Because the left side of Balance D in Figure 4.5 is now the same as the left of balance A of Figure 4.4, we know that one plate and two glasses balance a pitcher. Hence, the two pitchers in balance C of Figure 4.4 may be replaced with two plates and four glasses as shown in balance E of Figure 4.5. This solves the second sub-goal, which leads to the solution of the first sub-goal (shown in balance F of Figure 4.5), which leads to the solution of the original problem as shown in balance G of Figure 4.5.

As another illustration of the method of sub-goals, consider the Railroad Triangle Problem in Figure 4.6 on page 68. *Stop reading and try to solve the problem.*

There are no inferences that can be drawn from the givens or the operations, and there are a variety of ways to solve the problem, one of which is trial and error. However, because it is apparent that solving the problem will involve a series of moves, it is more useful to attempt to define one or more sub-goals before proceeding. *Stop reading and try to define one or more useful sub-goals.*

Because the goal requires that the positions of the two railroad cars be switched, one useful sub-goal is to find a way to reverse their relative positions (i.e., white on the left and black on the right) anyplace on the track.

In attacking this problem, it is best to represent the engine and car positions by making a schematic representation of the track on paper and choosing objects to represent the railroad cars and engine. Keep in mind that you must be able to tell which way the engine is facing. One way to attain the first sub-goal of getting the cars on opposite sides of each other is illustrated in Figure 4.7, where E represents the engine, W the white car, and Bl the black car. The steps are as follows: (1) Move the engine backward along AB past B; (2) move it up to the white car; (3) pull the white car backward past B; (4) push it along AB past A; (5) pull backward on AC and hook the black car on back of the engine; and (6) move the train forward past A.

Figure 4.6. Railroad Triangle Problem.

The main track AB and two small branches AD and BD form a railroad triangle. When a locomotive backs from A to B, goes forward into BD, and backs out of AD, it has reversed its direction on AB. But how does the engineer move the black car to BD and the white car to AD and return the locomotive to face left on AB? The dead end beyond the switch at C can hold only the locomotive or one car. The engine can push or pull with both ends.

At this point, the cars and engine could be repositioned as in the goal, but it requires turning the engine around once, thereby leaving it headed in the wrong direction. Of course, you would probably know this only by trying it once. In any event, you would then need to define a second sub-goal of turning the engine around without disturbing the relative positions of the cars. This can be accomplished by unhooking the cars outside the areas involved in

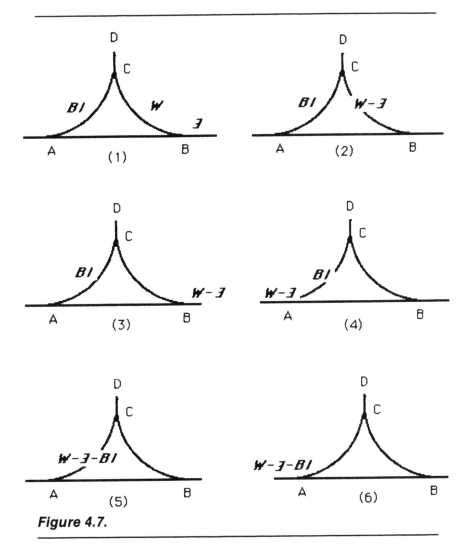

Figure 4.7.

ABD before repositioning them. Then, when the engine is turned around again during the repositioning of the cars, it will be facing the same way as in the beginning.

Looking at step 6 in Figure 4.7, you will see that the train is to the left of A with the white car hooked to the front of the engine, the black car on the back, and the engine facing to the left. The moves to accomplish the sub-goal of turning the engine around without disturbing the relative positions of the cars (shown in Figure 4.8) are as follows: (1) Unhook W (leaving it at the left of A) and push Bl backward beyond B and unhook it; (2) move E around BC to D; and

(3) go backward to A. E is now facing to the right as shown in Figure 4.8, and we are ready to work on the final sub-goal of repositioning the cars as specified in the goal. *If you have not already solved the problem, stop reading and try to do so.*

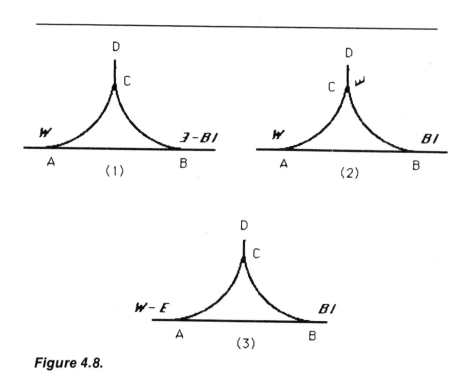

Figure 4.8.

One set of moves that will accomplish the final sub-goal (shown in Figure 4.9) is as follows: (1) Move E backward along A and hook onto W at the back of E; (2) move E along AB, leave W between A and B, move E beyond B, and hook it onto B1; (3) pull B1 up BC, leave it between B and C (goal position), and move E backward to D; (4) move E down beyond A; (5) back E along AB, hook onto W, and pull it back beyond A; and (6) push W backward along AC, leave it between A and C (goal position), move E beyond A, and finally back E between A and B (goal position).

In this solution, three sub-goals were defined: (1) moving the cars to sides opposite from what they were at the beginning, (2) turning the engine around, and (3) repositioning the cars. One could, of course, call each movement on one part of the track a sub-goal. The choice of the sub-goal and its size are determined by the person solving the problem. The important thing is to realize

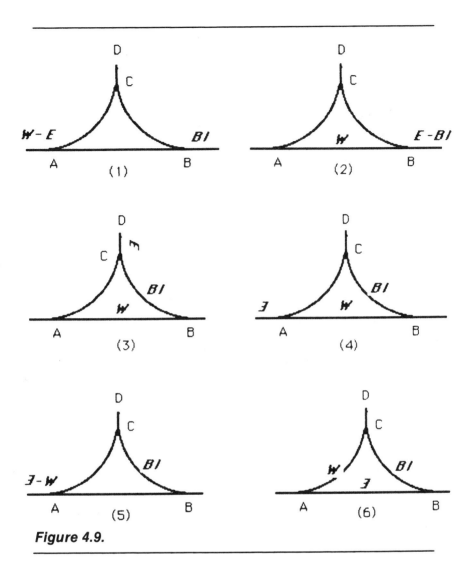

Figure 4.9.

that you can more easily solve the sub-goal or sub-problem than the problem as a whole, and that is what makes the method of sub-goals so useful.

SUB-GOALS WITH RECURSIVE RELATIONSHIPS

We next turn to an application of the sub-goal strategy in problems where there are recursive relationships among the elements of the problem. In such problems, the goal is the sum of smaller similar sub-goals, each of which is the sum of yet smaller similar sub-goals. Thus, the strategy for solving the entire problem is to work backward from the goal by forming smaller sub-goals until the beginning is reached and the smallest sub-goal is easy to solve. The successive sub-goals are then combined to reach the goal. As an example, consider the A Maze Problem in Figure 4.10. *Stop reading and try to solve the problem by breaking it into a series of successively smaller sub-goals.*

Figure 4.10. A Maze Problem.

A mouse enters a maze in search of a piece of cheese. There are infinitely many paths the mouse could follow, but only a finite number will lead the mouse closer to the goal with every step. How many such paths are there?

At first one might be tempted to solve the problem simply by tracing all the distinct routes from the beginning to the cheese and then adding them up. However, this soon becomes very tedious and is also difficult to keep organized. A much better way is to make use of the recursive relationships among the various intersections, or points. If you analyze the problem carefully, you will recognize that the number of routes from the start to any point is simply the sum of the number of routes from the start through all intersections leading directly into the point in question. For example, the number of routes leading to intersection I of Figure 4.11 is the sum of routes from the start to intersections E and H. There is one route from the start to H and three from the start to E (one direct, one through D, and one through A). Thus, there are four routes from the start to point I, which you can easily verify by tracing them.

Of course, we are only considering routes that travel diagonally (where there are diagonal paths) or up or to the right, not detours that go down or to the left. There are two amazing things about solving the problem this way. The first is that it is really unnecessary to trace all the routes in order to count them, and the second is that almost anyone could solve the problem this way in less than five minutes. It is simply a matter of determining the number of routes to each intersection by working from the start to the upper right until you know how many routes there are to points J, K, and N, which

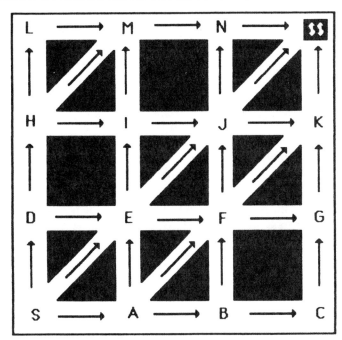

Figure 4.11.

lead directly to the goal. As the problem is stated, there are fifty-three different paths the rat could take to the cheese. The number of paths from the start to each point is shown in Figure 4.12.

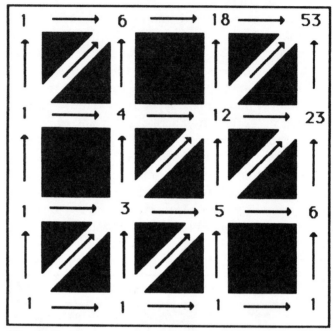

Figure 4.12.

As a more complex example of a problem with recursive relationships, consider the Tower of Hanoi problem in Figure 4.13. *Stop reading the text, read the problem, and try to solve it.*

In analyzing the problem you will find that there are no additional inferences that can be made about the givens or the operations. The problem is simply a matter of finding the fewest number of moves needed to transfer the six discs to an empty peg within the stated restrictions. Most people attempt to solve this problem with the method of trial and error, but because there are so many possible combinations of moves, the task becomes very difficult. However, the appropriate use of the method of sub-goals turns the problem into a much simpler one, where most of the effort is involved in keeping track of progress toward the goal. Also, contrary to what it would appear at the outset, determining the number of moves necessary to solve the problem is considerably

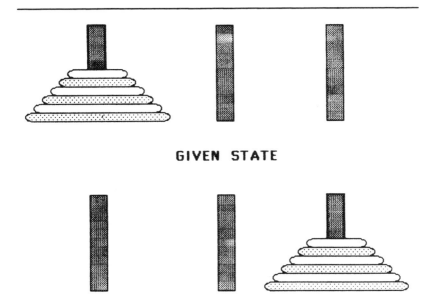

GIVEN STATE

GOAL STATE

Figure 4.13. Tower of Hanoi Problem.

The object of the pyramid puzzle is to transfer the six discs from the starting peg to one of the empty pegs, according to the following rules: (1) you may move only one disc at a time, and (2) you may never place a disc on top of one that is smaller than it. What is the smallest number of moves that can be used to transfer the six discs from the starting peg to one of the empty ones?

easier than generating the actual moves in the correct sequence. The latter problem is very unwieldy if you do not have the discs and pegs at hand. Without the pegs and discs, one way to keep track of the information generated in the problem is to draw a diagram similar to Figure 4.13, where the pegs are labeled A, B, and C and the discs are numbered 1 through 6, with 1 being the smallest and 6 being the largest. Assume the goal is to move the discs from A to C following the rules given. *Stop reading and try to solve the problem by defining a series of recursive sub-goals.*

You can solve the Tower of Hanoi Problem by defining a set of recursive sub-goals, and then breaking each of those into smaller sub-goals. This process is continued until you have generated a large set of trivial problems to be solved. You do, of course, need to systematically record the sub-goals so they can be combined for the complete solution. The first set of sub-goals can be defined by noting that the movement of discs 1-6 from A to C is composed of three sub-goals. The first is to move discs 1-5 from A to B, thereby uncovering disk 6. The second sub-goal is simply a move of disc 6 from A to C. The third sub-goal is to move discs 1-5 from B to C on top of disk 6. Thus, the 6-disc problem can be divided into two 5-disc problems and one movement of disc 6.

Although the 5-disc problems still are not trivial, I hope you can now see that each of the two 5-disc problems can be divided further into two 4-disc problems and one appropriate movement of disc 5. For example, the movement of discs 1-5 from A to B involves moving discs 1-4 from A to C, moving disc 5 from A to B, and moving discs 1-4 from C to B. Therefore, the 6-disc problem can now be conceptualized as four 4-disc problems (two for each 5-disc problem), two movements of disc 5, and one movement of disc 6.

As you continue to define sub-goals in this fashion, you will find that each disc problem can be subdivided into two smaller problems using one fewer disc plus the movement of the larger disc. Thus, each of the four 4-disc problems becomes two 3-disc problems, plus a movement of disc 4. In turn, we can convert the eight 3-disc problems into two 2-disc problems, which results in sixteen 2-disc problems, plus eight movements of disc 3. Finally, the 2-disc problems can be converted into 32 1-disc problems consisting of one movement of disc 1. In all, there will be thirty-two movements of disc 1, sixteen movements of disc 2, eight movements of disc 3, four movements of disc 4, two movements of disc 5, and one movement of disc 6, making a total of sixty-three movements to attain the goal. The Tower of Hanoi Problem is an excellent demonstration of the power of the method of recursive sub-goals on a problem for which its use is not immediately obvious but where it simplifies the solution greatly. Of course, it should be noted once again that determining the number of disc movements is a different problem from determining the exact sequence of those sixty-three movements.

SUMMARY

It is often quite natural to try to break a problem into smaller parts and try to solve one part at a time rather than tackle the whole thing at once. However, I have argued in this chapter that often there is something additional to be gained from being very conscious and deliberate about doing that. It is especially helpful to carefully analyze the givens in an attempt to find the best or most appropriate sub-goals. It should be noted that although I have talked about the *method* of sub-goals, defining useful sub-goals usually is not sufficient for solving a problem. Most frequently, one or more of the other methods is used to solve the sub-goals.

A particularly powerful aspect of sub-goals can be shown in cases where recursive relationships are present. In these cases, the problem can be subdivided into a set of smaller, but similar sub-problems. This process is repeated until a set of small sub-problems is created that is easily solved. Once the set of resulting sub-goals is reached, they are combined to form a complete solution to the problem.

Practice Problems

PRINTER'S INK

To number the pages of a large book requires 2,989 digits. How many pages are there in the book?

THE MONGOLIAN RAILWAY SYSTEM

The Mongolian Railway System suffers from a shortage of track. Occasionally, the whole system comes to a halt when two large trains meet at a switching area where the siding is too small. For example, every Thursday a fifty-car passenger train and a fifty-car freight train meet at an area built to accommodate twenty-five-car trains. The siding is connected to the main track at both ends. The engines can push or pull with both ends. Can you figure out how they get past each other?

GRUNDY'S GAME

Two players begin play with a single stack of seven checkers. The first player divides the stack into two stacks that must be *unequal.* Each player alternately thereafter divides any stack into two unequal piles. Thus, a pile of four can be converted into piles of three and one, but a pile of one or two is unplayable. The winner is the last player able to make a legal move. Can you find a strategy that will always guarantee a win?

A TRAIN ENCOUNTER

Two trains, each with eighty cars, must pass on a single track that has a dead-end siding. How can they pass when the siding is large enough only for an engine and forty cars?

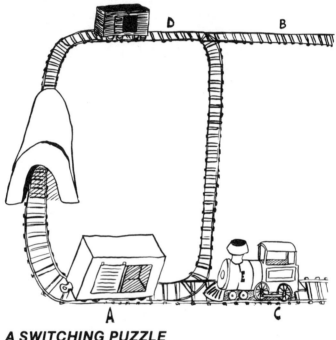

A
C

A SWITCHING PUZZLE

The tunnel is wide enough to accommodate the locomotive but not wide enough for either car. The problem is to use the locomotive for switching the positions of the two cars, and then return the locomotive to its original spot. Each end of the locomotive can be used for pushing or pulling, and the two cars may, if desired, be coupled to each other. For an extra challenge remove the top siding. Two additional moves are required to solve the problem.

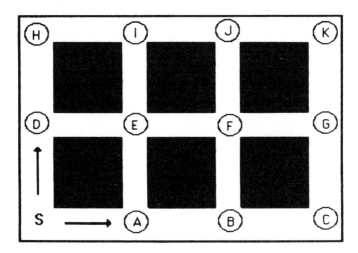

Map 1

ROUTES

In the accompanying map, fill in the circles at each corner with the maximum number of different paths that you can find from S to that corner going only in the direction of the arrows.

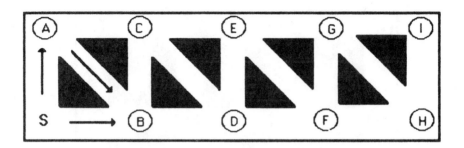

Map 2

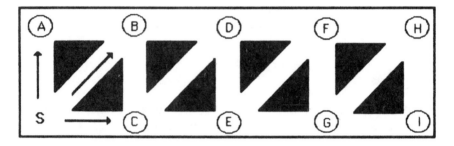

Map 3

In these maps, fill in the circles at each corner with the maximum number of different paths that you can find from S to that corner going only in the direction of the arrows.

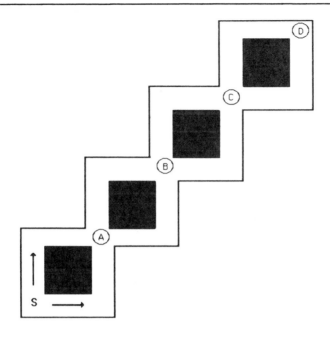

Map 4

In this map, calculate the number of distinct routes from S to each circle and record your results.

5
Contradiction

Try to solve the problem in Figure 5.1.

Figure 5.1. Whodunit?

Four men, one of whom is known to have committed a certain crime, said the following when questioned by an inspector from Scotland Yard.

> *Growley:* "Snavely did it."
> *Snavely:* "Gaston did it."
> *Gus:* "I didn't do it."
> *Gaston:* "Snavely lied when he said I did it."

If only one of these four statements is true, whodunit?

If you find yourself confused and unable to make any progress, you will probably benefit from a discussion of the problem-solving method called *contradiction*. As with every problem, we must have firmly in mind the givens, goals, and operations. The givens are explicitly stated here (reread the foregoing statements) as well as the goal (find out who did it). There are only four possible solutions to the problem: Growley, Snavely, Gus, or Gaston. In applying the method of contradiction we assume each of the suspects, one at a time, is guilty and test to see which assumption is consistent with the givens. For example, if we assume that Growley is the guilty one, is this consistent with the four statements given by the suspects? *Stop reading and check the four statements assuming Growley did it.*

You need to make a table to keep track of the information— remember the three Rs, record, record, record. One way to do this is shown in Table 5.1. Across the top are each of the suspects. Down the side are each of the statements made by the four men. Assuming that Growley is guilty, the four statements are examined and marked true or false.

Table 5.1. Partial solution to the Whodunit Problem.

STATEMENTS	THE CULPRITS			
	Growley	Snavely	Gus	Gaston
Growley: "Snavely did it."	F			
Snavely: "Gaston did it."	F			
Gus: "I didn't do it."	T			
Gaston: "Snavely lied when he said I did it."	T			

Clearly, if Growley did it then two of the four statements would have to be true, but we were given the condition that only one is true. Thus, the assumption that Growley did it has led to a contradiction that eliminates him from consideration. *Stop reading and apply the same reasoning to the other three suspects.*

The problem-solving strategy of contradiction is especially useful when the answer is restricted to a small number of possibilities and when it is difficult or impossible to directly prove the correct answer. By systematically testing each possible answer against the given information, we reject those that are inconsistent (contradict the givens) and select those that satisfy all conditions of the problem. Is it possible that more than one answer is acceptable? Yes! Does this mean that the method is faulty? No! It only means that the conditions of the problem are not sufficient to produce a unique answer. The method of contradiction is also valuable in other ways. It selects all possible answers, and if there are no answers it indicates that too. The completed chart for the Whodunit problem is found in Table 5.2.

Table 5.2. Complete solution to the Whodunit Problem.

STATEMENTS	THE CULPRITS			
	Growley	Snavely	Gus	Gaston
Growley: "Snavely did it."	F	T	F	F
Snavely: "Gaston did it."	F	F	F	T
Gus: "I didn't do it."	T	T	F	T
Gaston: "Snavely lied when he said I did it."	T	T	T	F

If Snavely did it then three statements are true—contradiction (only one can be true). If Gaston did it then two statements are true—again a contradiction. If Gus did it then one statement is true, and that is consistent with the given conditions of the problem. So, Gus is our man. Trivial, my dear Watson, trivial!

Keeping track of information symbolically, graphically, by a chart, or in some systematic way cannot be overemphasized. Except for the simplest problems, any search for a solution is made considerably easier when we take the load off our memory and record what we know on paper. As discussed earlier in Chapter 1, it helps us recognize many conditions at a glance and work at a level beyond the limitations of our memory.

As another example of the method of contradiction, consider the problem in Figure 5.2 on page 88. *Stop reading and search for your own solution.*

Figure 5.2. The Finelli's Finis Problem.

Shorty Finelli was found shot to death one morning and the police, with better-than-average luck, had three red-hot suspects behind bars by nightfall. That evening the men were questioned and made the following statements:

Buck: (1) "I didn't do it."
      (2) "I never saw Joey before."
      (3) "Sure, I know Shorty."
Joey: (1) "I didn't do it."
      (2) "Buck and Tippy are both pals of mine."
      (3) "Buck never killed anybody."
Tippy: (1) "I didn't do it."
      (2) "Buck lied when he said he'd never seen Joey before."
      (3) "I don't know who did it."

If one and only one of each man's statements is false, and if one of the men is guilty, who is the murderer?

Here the need to record information in some systematic way is even more acute. We now have three statements from each person to verify. Our first problem is deciding on a good way to record the information. One way is illustrated in Table 5.3.

Table 5.3. Table for recording the Finelli's Finis Problem.

STATEMENTS	SUSPECTS		
	Buck	Joey	Tippy
1	?	?	?
2	?	?	?
3	?	?	?

Across the top are suspects and down the side are statement numbers. Assuming one of the suspects is guilty, we can test three statements for each man and indicate whether they are true or false and check the results with the givens for consistency. Because one and only one of each suspect's statements is false, our table must have one false (F) and two true (T) statements in each column. If not, we have contradicted the givens and must conclude that the one we assumed guilty is not. There are three possible culprits so the worst we can expect is to fill out the table three times, once for each man. *Stop reading and fill out the table, assuming that Tippy is guilty.*

If we assume that Tippy did it, then his first statement is false, requiring the other two to be true (remember, only one of three can be false). But this leads us to a contradiction right away because Tippy must know himself, so statement three (I don't know who did it) is also false. Cross out Tippy from the list of suspects. *Stop reading and fill out the table assuming that Buck is guilty.*

If Buck is guilty, then his first statement is false so the other two are true. So far so good. Now move on to the statements of the other suspects. Joey's third statement must be false, so the other two are true. Is the information consistent so far? No. If both Buck and Joey's second statements are true, they contradict each other. One says they know each other and the other says they don't. So again we arrive at a contradiction, which clears Buck of the crime. Because someone is the culprit and Joey is the only remaining candidate, we apparently have our man. But let's make certain this problem is well posed. Assuming that Joey did it does not lead to any contradictions. The completed table is shown in Table 5.4.

Table 5.4 *The solution to The Finelli's Finis Problem.*

STATEMENTS	SUSPECTS		
	Buck	Joey	Tippy
1	T	F	T
2	F	T	T
3	T	T	F

If no further examples were available, you might get the impression that contradiction is useful only for solving puzzles—especially those of the "whodunit" variety. That would be a reasonable inference, but fortunately it is false. The method of contradiction is frequently used in other ways. For example, consider the following statement:

If the product of two whole numbers is greater than 65, then one of the numbers must be larger than 8.

Stop reading and decide whether this statement is true or false.

If the conclusion in this statement is false, what can we say about the two whole numbers? Clearly, both of the numbers must be smaller than or equal to 8. But this would imply that the product is at most 64, contradicting the condition that the product of the two numbers is greater than 65. Because the only other alternative to the original conclusion is not possible, we must conclude that the statement is true.

PROVING MATHEMATICAL THEOREMS

One of the most elegant applications of the method of contradiction was given by Euclid in the third century B.C. He proved that among the natural numbers 1, 2, 3, 4 . . . an infinite number of them must be prime. A prime number is one that cannot be written as the product of two integers other than itself and one. For example, 2, 3, 5, 7, 11, and 13 are all prime numbers. Euclid's proof is one of the first recorded uses of the method of contradiction. To prove that there must be an infinite number of primes, Euclid assumed the opposite—there are only finitely many primes—and outlined the consequences of this assumption:

1. There is a largest prime P.

2. Any number larger than P is not prime.

3. $N = (1 \cdot 2 \cdot 3 \ldots \cdot P) + 1$ is larger than P and thus is not prime.

4. By 3, N has a prime factor q.

5. The prime q is smaller than P and thus by 3, $N = (1 \cdot 2 \cdot 3 \cdot \ldots q \ldots \cdot P) + 1 = (r \cdot q) + 1$.

6. But if $N = (r \cdot q) + 1$, then q is not a factor of N.

Statements 4 and 6 contradict each other because by statement 4, q is a factor of N and by statement 6, q is not a factor of N. Thus, the assumption that there is a largest prime leads to a contradiction, and the only alternative—there are an infinite number of primes—is true. You may have found this example difficult to follow. In spite of that, it does illustrate the power of the method of contradiction in proving important theorems in mathematics. Even though you probably won't prove many theorems, I hope you will find the method useful in solving problems you do encounter.

SUMMARY

The method of contradiction is useful in situations for which there are a relatively small number of alternative solutions, and they are known. The goal is to determine the correct one, if there is a unique alternative. This is accomplished by assuming each of the alternatives, in turn, and testing their implications against the givens.

The testing of the alternatives involves considerable use of inference, as discussed in Chapter 2. If there is a unique solution to the problem, all but one of the alternatives will lead to logical contradictions with the givens. Thus, from a logical perspective, if there is a correct solution, and only one is consistent with all the given information, then it must be the correct one.

Although it was not discussed explicitly earlier, I would like to point out the contradiction is useful in conjunction with other methods. In many cases it is possible to exclude some of the potential solutions to a problem by inference before using contradiction. Finally, it is probably true that contradiction is not as widely applicable as the other methods that have been discussed, but it can be very effective in those situations to which it does apply.

Practice Problems

TRUTH & FALSEHOOD

In a faraway land there dwelt two tribes of people. The Ananias were inveterate liars, and the Diogenes were unfailingly veracious. Once upon a time a stranger visited the land, and on meeting a party of three inhabitants inquired to what tribe they belonged. The first murmured something that the stranger did not catch. The second remarked, "He said he was an Anania." The third said to the second, "You're a liar!" Now the question is, of what tribe was the third person?

I'VE BEEN POISONED

Four men were eating dinner together in a restaurant when one of them struggled to his feet, cried out, "I've been poisoned," and fell dead. His companions were arrested on the spot and under questioning made the following statements, exactly one of which is false in each case.

Watts: "I didn't do it."
"I was sitting next to O'Neil."
"We had our usual waiter today."

Rogers: "I was sitting across the table from Smith."
"We had a new waiter today."
"The waiter didn't do it."

O'Neil: "Rogers didn't do it."
"It was the waiter who poisoned Smith."
"Watts lied when he said we had our usual waiter today."

Assuming that only Smith's companions and the waiter are implicated, who was the murderer?

A CRIME STORY

An elementary school teacher had her purse stolen. The thief had to be Lillian, Judy, David, Theo, or Margaret. When questioned, each child made three statements:

Lillian: (1) "I didn't take the purse."
(2) "I have never in my life stolen anything."
(3) "Theo did it."

Judy: (4) "I didn't take the purse."

(5) "My daddy is rich enough, and I have a purse of my own."

(6) "Margaret knows who did it."

David: (7) "I didn't take the purse."

(8) "I didn't know Margaret before I enrolled in this school."

(9) "Theo did it."

Theo: (10) "I am not guilty."

(11) "Margaret did it."

(12) "Lillian is lying when she says I stole the purse."

Margaret: (13) "I didn't take the teacher's purse."

(14) "Judy is guilty."

(15) "David can vouch for me because he has known me since I was born."

Later, each child admitted that two of his statements were true and one was false. Assuming this is true, who stole the purse?

VICE VERSA

Things are not always what they seem. What is true from one point of view may be false from another and vice versa, and here is a puzzle to prove it. Undoubtedly, every arithmetic teacher in the land would unhesitatingly declare that it is incorrect to write the following:

$$
\begin{array}{r}
S\ E\ V\ E\ N \\
-\ N\ I\ N\ E \\
\hline
E\ I\ G\ H\ T
\end{array}
$$

It is nonetheless true in this puzzle, in which each letter represents a different digit. It is correct subtraction, and in fact it can be successfully decoded in two quite different ways. What digits do the various letters stand for in each of the two possible solutions?

THREE BOYS

Three boys weigh a total of 250 pounds, of which Bill weighs 105 pounds. The barefoot boy weighs exactly 15 pounds less than the heaviest boy. Chuck weighs more than the boy with sneakers on. Art weighs less than the boy with loafers on. Which boy is barefoot?

WIRE MONEY

A college student sent the following message to her father:

$$
\begin{array}{r}
\$\ W\ I\ R\ E \\
+\ M\ O\ R\ E \\
\hline
\$\ M\ O\ N\ E\ Y
\end{array}
$$

If each letter represents a unique digit (0-9), how much should her dad send?

FATHERS AND SONS

Three women, Beth, Dorothy, and Louise, are married to three men, Barber, Cutler, and Drake. Each couple has a son, the names of the boys being Allan, Henry, and Victor. From the information given below, identify each married couple and their son.

1. Drake is neither Louise's husband nor Henry's father.
2. Beth is neither Cutler's wife nor Allan's mother.
3. If Allan's father is either Cutler or Drake, then Louise is Victor's mother.
4. If Louise is Cutler's wife, Dorothy is not Allan's mother.

Working
Backward

Try to solve the problem in Figure 6.1.

Figure 6.1. The Matching Coins Problem.

Three people agree to match coins for money. They each flip a coin, and the one who fails to match the other two is the loser. The loser must double the amount of money that each opponent has at that time. After three games, each player has lost once and has $24. How much did each person have in the beginning?

Any solution to a problem can be thought of as a path that leads from the given information to the goal. In some cases, what is typically thought of as the goal is already known, and the problem lies in determining the correct set of operations that will accomplish the goal or the initial state from which the goal was derived. In these situations it is frequently easier to start at the goal and work backward to the initial state. Once this is accomplished, the solution is simply either the initial state or the same series of steps in reverse. For example, in the Matching Coins Problem, the end result is known—all three players finish with $24. The initial state can be found by working backward one game at a time. Specifically, because each player had $24 after the third game, the two winners of this game (who doubled their money) must have had $12 each at the end of the second game. In order to pay each winner $12 and still end up with $24, the loser of this game must have had $48. Thus, the distribution of money among the three players after the second game has been determined. In a similar fashion, we can continue working backward to reach the initial state.

If we let P1, P2, and P3 represent the players who lost the first, second, and third games, respectively, then Table 6.1 shows the distribution of money among the three players at each stage constructed by working backward.

Table 6.1. Solution to the Matching Coins Problem.

STATES	PLAYERS		
	P1	P2	P3
After 3rd game	$24	$24	$24
After 2nd game	$12	$12	$48
After 1st game	$ 6	$42	$24
Beginning	$39	$21	$12

Note that in the problem the path from the goal back to the initial state is uniquely determined; thus, at each state in the solution the previous state is forced upon us by the conditions of the problem. By working backward, we were able to arrive at the solution directly without any detours.

The Coffee with Your Milk Problem from Chapter 2 is very simple to solve with a working backward strategy. Recall that the problem begins with two cups of liquid—coffee in one cup and milk in the other. A teaspoon of milk is transferred to the coffee cup and mixed. Then a teaspoon of the diluted coffee is transferred back to the milk and mixed. The problem is to determine if there is more milk in the coffee cup than there is coffee in the milk cup or if the amount of milk in the coffee equals the amount of coffee in the milk. The amazing thing about this problem is that we can continue to trade teaspoons of diluted milk and diluted coffee indefinitely, and the answer remains the same as long as we always trade teaspoon for teaspoon and maintain the same amount of liquid in each cup. *Stop reading and try to solve this problem by working backward.*

If we were to keep track of the amount of milk or coffee being transferred in each exchange, the problem quickly gets out of hand. However, if we go immediately to the end result—two cups of liquid—a simple observation solves this problem. Suppose the milk and coffee were to separate and the milk rose to the top of each cup, as illustrated in Figure 6.2.

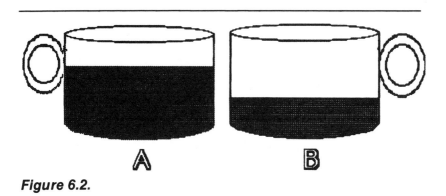

Figure 6.2.

Because we began with a full cup of coffee and a full cup of milk, the coffee in cup B must be exactly equal to the milk in cup A. That is, they simply replaced each other. Thus, the concentration of milk in cup A is exactly the same as the concentration of coffee in cup B, and the problem is solved.

The Wimbledon Problem in Figure 6.3 is another example in which jumping ahead to the end result and looking backward makes the problem extremely easy to solve. *Stop reading and try to solve this problem.*

After the tournament is over there is only one person who won every match (the winner, of course). Everyone else (one hundred players) lost exactly once, because it is a single-elimination tourna-

Figure 6.3. The Wimbledon Problem.

One hundred and one eager tennis players entered the Wimbledon tennis tournament this year. How many matches were played in all before a champion was crowned? Remember, Wimbledon is a single-elimination tournament.

ment. In every game one person lost, so the number of games played was exactly one hundred.

A practical, everyday situation for which working backward is useful arises when you have something scheduled at a particular time, but you have several other tasks to accomplish prior to that. You first make a list of the things that have to be done, the order, and an estimate of the time each will take. Then, beginning with the time you need to leave for the scheduled event, you can work backward to see when each event will need to be started.

As an example of a scheduling problem, let's assume you are going to a concert that begins at 7:00 P.M. The other things that need to be accomplished and their estimated times are: drive to the concert—thirty minutes, shower and get dressed—one hour, prepare and eat dinner—thirty minutes, wash some clothes and write some long overdue letters—forty-five minutes, and wash the car—forty-five minutes. Working backward from the 7:00 starting time of the concert, you would need to leave at 6:30, begin your shower at 5:30, begin dinner at 5:00, wash clothes and write letters at 4:15, and wash the car at 3:30. Thus, you can see that if the estimated times are realistic and you want to accomplish all the things on your list, you will need to begin at 3:30.

SUMMARY

Working backward is most useful for problems where we already know what would usually be considered the goal, but we don't know the set of operations that will produce the goal or perhaps the initial state. Although it is sometimes possible to solve the problem working forward through a long process of trial and error, working backward can simplify the solution tremendously.

As with contradiction, although the strategy of working backward is a very powerful one, it probably isn't used as frequently as some of the other strategies we've discussed. It is somewhat like coming out of a late movie only to find that you forgot to turn out the lights on your car and the battery is dead. Having a set of jumper cables right then would be like the working-backward strategy. You don't use them very often, but when you need them nothing else will do.

Practice Problems

THREE SAILORS AND A MONKEY

Three sailors and a monkey were on an island. One evening the sailors rounded up all the coconuts they could find and put them in one large pile. Being exhausted from working so hard, they decided to wait and divide them up equally in the morning. During the night, a sailor awoke and separated the nuts into three equal piles, with one coconut left over, which he gave to the monkey. He took one pile, buried it, pushed the other two together and went back to his hammock. He was followed in turn by the other two sailors, each of whom did exactly the same thing. The next morning the remaining nuts were divided equally among the sailors with one remaining nut, which was given to the monkey. What is the least number of coconuts they could have collected?

TRAINED PIGEON

Two trains, 120 miles apart, are racing toward each other on a collision course, each at a speed of 30 miles per hour. A bird flies continuously at a speed of 75 miles per hour between the smoke stacks of each train, making instantaneous reversals at each end. This continues right up until the two trains collide, leaving a pile of crumpled steel and a few feathers. How far did the bird fly?

GURU

One day while in meditation, a guru fell to the bottom of a 30-foot well. After watching his attempts to get out, it was determined that each day the Guru climbed up 3 feet and each night he slid back 2 feet. How long did it take the guru to get out?

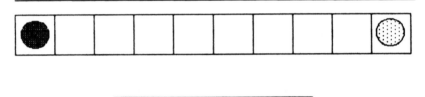

Figure 6.4. THE WOOLWORTH GAME

One player has dark checkers and the other has light checkers. Both sets of checkers are part of the game, and either set can be used to make a move. Take turns advancing or retreating one of the checkers as many spaces as you wish. "Jumping" is not allowed, so when one player moves a checker adjacent to an opponent's checker, the opponent must move back toward the starting position. The player who forces an opponent to move back into the original position on both sets of squares wins the game. Take turns going first. Find the winning strategy for going first or second.

TRUCK IN THE DESERT

A truck reaches the edge of a desert 400 miles wide. The vehicle averages only 1 mile to the gallon of gas, and the total available gasoline capacity, including extra cans, is 180 gallons; so gasoline dumps will have to be established in the desert. There is ample gas to be had at the desert's edge. With wise planning of the operation, what is the least gas consumption necessary to get the vehicle across the desert?

NIM

Two players alternate picking up one, two, or three pennies from a pile of twelve pennies. The player who takes the last coin from the pile is the loser. Find a winning strategy for the person who goes first or second.

Solutions
to Practice
Problems

CHAPTER 1

Tug-of-War

There are three basic relationships that can be established from the information, using the first letters of the names as symbols. They are: (1) M > S + K, (2) M + S = K + A, and (3) M + K < S + A. From there, it can be shown logically that Angie is stronger than Marie, who is stronger than Susan, who, in turn, is stronger than Karen.

The Dairy Farm

The key is to symbolize the givens and to establish the relationships among them. The overall relationship that is important in this problem is that the amount of milk given by the two groups of cows is equal, even though one group takes five days and the other group takes only four days. Because the two amounts of milk are equal, the basic relationship can be stated symbolically as:

$$5 \text{ days} \times (4Bl + 3Br) = 4 \text{ days} \times (3bl + 5Br)$$

Carrying out the multiplication, you get:

$$20Bl + 15Br = 12Bl + 20Br$$

At this point, you can imagine the two groups of cows standing on two sides of a large weighing scale. Because the twenty brown cows on the right side need only twelve black cows to balance, but the twenty black cows on the left need fifteen additional brown cows to balance, the brown cows must give more milk.

Trains

This is a difficult problem for many people. First it is important to get an understanding of the two situations where (1) the passenger train is overtaking the freight train when the trains are going in the same direction, and (2) where the passenger train is passing the freight train when they are going in opposite directions. This can be accomplished either by drawing some diagrams or by using some physical objects that can be moved about. From a careful analysis of the two situations, it can be concluded that the time required for the passenger train to overtake the freight train is a function of the *difference* in the speeds of the two trains. However, the time required for them to pass when they meet head-on is a function of the *sum* of their speeds. Furthermore, as stated in the problem, the relationship between the times for the two events is 2 to 1. That is, the sum of their speeds is twice the difference in their speeds. Stated symbolically, $(F + P) = 2(F - P)$.

With the appropriate relationships established, the problem could easily be solved algebraically, but it is instructive to attempt to solve it conceptually and logically. At this point, it really doesn't matter that we are dealing with speeds. The problem can be thought of as a general case of seeking the relationship between any two quantities when their *sum* is exactly twice their *difference*. After some careful thought and some helpful diagrams, it can be shown that the ratio is 3 to 1. That is, the speed of the passenger train is three times that of the freight train.

Reverse

The best way to represent this problem is to get some pieces of paper with the numbers drawn on so you can manipulate them more easily. One solution is $4231 \longrightarrow 3241 \longrightarrow 2341 \longrightarrow 4321 \longrightarrow 1234$.

Three Moves

The best way to represent this problem is to actually use the match sticks or some other objects that can be manipulated directly. Given some actual objects to manipulate, a solution is reasonably straightforward as the following table indicates:

Table S.1. Solution to the Three Moves Problem.

MOVES	STACKS		
	1	2	3
Begin	11	6	7
Move 1	4	6	14
Move 2	4	12	8
Move 3	8	8	8

Counting Squares

The key to this problem is to make a table to keep track of the number of squares of various unit sizes of two, three, four, and five. A relationship can then be inferred from the results that will enable the prediction to be made for the six-unit square. The complete solution is as follows:

Table S.2. Solution to the Counting Squares Problem.

UNIT SIZE	NUMBER OF N-UNIT SQUARES						TOTAL
	1	2	3	4	5	6	
2 × 2	4	1					5
3 × 3	9	4	1				14
4 × 4	16	9	4	1			30
5 × 5	25	16	9	4	1		55
6 × 6	36	25	16	9	4	1	91

Twenty

The total number of combinations is eleven. Here it is important to find a way to systematically determine all the possibilities without missing any so that you can be certain that you have included all of the legal combinations and no illegal ones. One such approach is to begin with the largest value possible for the digit beginning at one side (*e.g.*, the left). Then "shift" values to other digits to the right, always keeping the values to the left as large as possible. A solution using such a strategy is as follows:

Table S.3. Solution to the Twenty Problem.

1.	13 + 1 + 1 + 1 + 1 + 1 + 1 + 1 = 20
2.	11 + 3 + 1 + 1 + 1 + 1 + 1 + 1 = 20
3.	9 + 5 + 1 + 1 + 1 + 1 + 1 + 1 = 20
4.	9 + 3 + 3 + 1 + 1 + 1 + 1 + 1 = 20
5.	7 + 7 + 7 + 1 + 1 + 1 + 1 + 1 = 20
6.	7 + 5 + 3 + 1 + 1 + 1 + 1 + 1 = 20
7.	7 + 3 + 3 + 3 + 1 + 1 + 1 + 1 = 20
8.	5 + 5 + 5 + 1 + 1 + 1 + 1 + 1 = 20
9.	5 + 5 + 3 + 3 + 1 + 1 + 1 + 1 = 20
10.	5 + 3 + 3 + 3 + 3 + 1 + 1 + 1 = 20
11.	3 + 3 + 3 + 3 + 3 + 3 + 1 + 1 = 20

Bell Hop

The most interesting aspect of this problem is that it is a classic example of a convincing argument that can lead one down the proverbial primrose path. Thus, in solving it, you must be careful to keep track of whose perspective is being used to account for a particular amount of money. For example, once the bell hop has given the customers back their money, then only $27 dollars has been paid for the room, not $29. The manager has $25 and the bell hop has $2. The deception is created in the way the last two sentences of the problem are written. At first reading, you may be persuaded to add the bell hop's tip to the $27 that the customers have paid for the room rather than subtracting it, and that leaves $1 of the original $30 unaccounted for. In terms of the original $30 paid for the room, the manager has $25, the bell hop has $2, and the customers each have $1, making a total of $30.

Change

As with the Twenty Problem, you must be careful to find a systematic way to list all the possibilities without leaving out any legal ones and not including any illegal ones. One way is to begin with as many dimes as possible, then nickels, and then pennies, systematically generating each new possibility using as many coins as possible of the highest value before proceeding to lower coins. There are twelve different ways change can be made. One way to show the solution is as follows:

	DIMES	NICKLES	PENNIES
1.	2	1	0
2.	2	0	5
3.	1	3	0
4.	1	2	5
5.	1	1	10
6.	1	0	15
7.	0	5	0
8.	0	4	5
9.	0	3	10
10.	0	2	15
11.	0	1	20
12.	0	0	25

Triangles

In this problem it is especially important to find a systematic way to isolate the different types of triangles to make certain that each one is counted once and only once. One approach is to reference triangles to a particular outside corner or side and count all triangles referenced to it. Then, because there are five outside corners or sides, there would be seven times that many triangles. Thus, there are a total of thirty-five different triangles. One way of organizing the solution is shown using the lower-left outside corner as a reference point, as in the illustration.

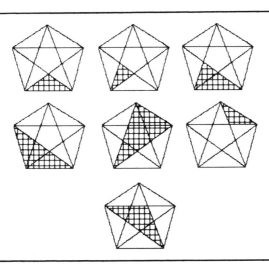

Lock Your Lockers

A representation is needed where the state of each locker can be changed from closed to open and vice versa. This could simply be a list of numbers with an O for open and an X for closed. The state can be changed by crossing out or erasing each time a new student goes through. With fifty or so lockers, a pattern emerges revealing that the lockers that remain open are those with numbers that are perfect squares (*e.g.*, 1, 4, 9, 16, 25, etc.).

Silver Dollars

The least there could be with ten pockets is 0, 1, 2, 3, 4, 5, 6, 7, 8, 9, which only sums to $45. Hence, the answer to the question is No!

CHAPTER 2 ·

Line Count

This problem is designed to provide skills in inferring a pattern in results obtained, while being careful to keep track of the information generated in the problem. It is very similar to the Counting Squares Problem in Chapter 1. The complete solution is as follows:

Table S.5. Solution to the
Line Count Problem.

POINTS	LINES
2	1
3	3
4	6
5	10
6	15
7	21
8	28
9	36

Diagonal Count

As with the Line Count Problem, this one is designed to provide skills in inferring a pattern in results while being careful to keep track of the information generated in the problem. The complete solution is as follows:

Table S.6. Solution to the
Diagonal Count Problem.

SIDES	DIAGONALS
3	0
4	2
5	5
6	9
7	14
8	20
9	27

Bottle's Volume

This problem is designed to test inferences about operations, in this case those that could be used for measuring and calculating volumes of bottles. It assumes that you are familiar with the formulas for calculating volumes of regular objects such as cylinders and cubes and that you could use a ruler to measure such quantities as the radius of a round bottle or the length of the sides of a rectangular bottle. It also involves what might be considered an insight regarding the movement of the liquid in the bottle if the orientation of the bottle is changed.

The total volume in any partially filled bottle is the sum of the liquid in the filled portion and the air in the unfilled portion. With the bottle upright, you can find the volume of the liquid by measuring the appropriate dimensions and using the appropriate formula, depending on whether the body of the bottle is round or rectangular. The critical inference is that you can then measure the volume of air in the unfilled portion by turning the bottle upside down and letting the liquid flow into the neck. No matter how irregular the neck, if the bottle is more than half full the liquid will still usually more than fill it. This will leave air only in the regular or cylindrical part of the bottle. The volume of air can be found as the liquid was by measuring the dimensions with the ruler and using the appropriate formula. The volume of air can now be added to the volume of the liquid found earlier, and the problem is solved.

Coffee with Your Milk

This problem creates difficulty for many people, not because they fail to be logical, but because they fail to consider all of the information in making their inferences. Most who have difficulty with the problem err in concluding that there is more milk in the coffee than coffee in the milk. They reason that the spoon of liquid first taken from the milk and put in the coffee was pure milk, but the spoon of liquid taken from the coffee and milk mixture is not pure coffee. Thus, they reason that more milk was put in the coffee than coffee was put in the milk.

It is true that a full spoon of milk was put in the coffee, and that less than a full spoon of coffee was put in the milk. However, because the coffee became a mixture, then part of the spoon of milk that was originally put in the coffee was taken back to the milk cup with the exchange. In fact, if you stop to analyze the contents of the

114

spoon of mixture before it was put into the milk, you will realize that the fraction of milk in it (*e.g.*, 1/10 spoon) must be the exact amount of coffee that would be needed to make it a spoon of pure coffee. Hence, if there is only 9/10 spoon of coffee in the spoon, then there is 1/10 spoon of milk being taken back. This means that only 9/10 spoon of milk was left in the coffee cup. Thus, once the mixture is put into the milk cup, there is the same amount of coffee in the milk as milk in the coffee.

The Reasoning of Age

As with some of the problems in Chapter 1, this problem is solved by using symbols and the given information to help analyze the relationships among the elements of the problem and then by using logic to determine the relative ages of all the people. The final solution is Steve > Jack = Stan > Bob > Kent > Karen.

Archimedes and His Pet Rock

This problem is a relatively straightforward example of analyzing the givens, which include some actual physics principles, and then making the correct inferences from those principles. First of all, while the rock was riding in the boat, it was floating and, according to the first principle, was displacing its weight of water. When it was thrown overboard and sank, according to the second principle, it then displaced less than its weight of water. Thus, the net effect was that the level in the lake fell because not as much water was being displaced when the rock was on the bottom of the lake as when it was riding in the boat.

The Tennis Player

This problem is an interesting combination of the use of a good representation (actually two representations) and sound reasoning. First, it is useful to make a chart listing the four people and the four sports so you can keep track of what the various people are not as well as what they are. Second, in this case it is helpful to have a diagram of a table to see what seating arrangements are possible and what restrictions those place on the assignment of people to sports. From statement 1 we can infer that Alice is not the swimmer and from statement 2 that Brian is not the gymnast. We know that Alice is not the gymnast, because statement 2 would put her across from

Brian, and that would not allow Carol and David to be sitting next to each other as statement 3 says they are. Thus, we now know that Alice is neither the swimmer nor the gymnast.

We can infer that Alice is not the skater, because that would make Carol the swimmer (from statement 1) and put her on Alice's left (from statement 4). This would then put David next to Carol (from statement 3) and across from Alice. The only position left for Brian would then be between Alice and David and across from Carol. However, that would require Carol to be the gymnast (from statement 2) instead of the swimmer (from statement 1). Because of this conflict, Alice can't be the skater. Because she is not the swimmer, the gymnast, nor the skater, she must be the tennis player, and the problem is solved. Just for practice, if you match up the rest of the people with their sports you will find that Carol is the gymnast, Brian is the swimmer, and David is the skater.

A Piece of Cake

This problem is a relatively straightforward example of good reasoning after a good analysis of the given information. The first inference is that there were five cakes baked because ten cups of flour were used and each cake required two cups. Then, because there were seven cups of sugar used, we can infer that there were two cakes that required two cups of sugar, making them German chocolate. The remaining three cakes were then white.

Gauss

This is another problem that focuses on inferences about the operations that could be used, and it could be considered an insight problem. As the story goes, Gauss noticed an interesting relationship between the numbers from 1 to 100. In particular, he realized that by starting at both ends of the set of numbers, pairs of numbers sum to 101. For example, $1 + 100, 2 + 99, 3 + 98 . . . 50 + 51$ each sum to 101. Because there are 50 of these pairs, the total is $50 \times 101 = 5050$. Not bad thinking for a schoolkid!

Two Trains

The important inference in this problem is the speeds of the trains relative to each other, rather than their absolute speeds. That is, the trains are approaching each other at a relative speed of 100 miles per hour. Because they travel that distance in an hour, they will be 100 miles apart an hour before they meet.

The Woodsman

This problem is one of the more difficult ones in the book for most people. First, it is very important to draw a diagram to represent the problem to make certain that you fully understand it and to help you keep track of the information you generate while solving it. The first important item to consider is that the woodsman traveled the same distance (twelve strokes) before meeting the oncoming ripples (relative to him) as he did afterward to catch the outgoing ripples. The goal then is to determine how much of the second twelve strokes was required to put the woodsman directly over the spot where the fish jumped.

An important inference is that because the ripples were going outward from the fish in all directions, the outgoing ripples traveled the same distance away from the fish as did the oncoming ripples before the woodsman met the oncoming ones. A second inference is that because the time was the same (the time for twelve strokes) until the woodsman caught the outgoing ripples, they traveled the same distance again before he caught them.

We now have enough information to conclude that the second twelve strokes traveled by the woodsman can be divided into three equal parts. The first part is that traveled by the oncoming ripples from the time they were created by the fish until the woodsman met them. The second part is that traveled by the outgoing ripples during the same time. The third part is the distance traveled by the outgoing ripples in the same additional time (the second twelve strokes) until the woodsman caught them. Thus the distance the oncoming ripples traveled until they were met by the woodsman is one-third of twelve, or four strokes. Those four strokes plus the first twelve traveled by the woodsman gives a total of sixteen strokes between the woodsman and the fish.

Cow, Goat, and Goose

This is also one of the most difficult problems in the book for most people. It also could be considered an insight problem. A critical step (the insight) is to conceptualize the growth of the pasture into two components. One is the growth that has accumulated prior to the animals being put in the pasture, and the other is the growth that continues each day. The pasture will last as long as it takes the animals to eat both components.

With the distinction between accumulated and daily growth in mind, you can begin to make inferences based on the information given. First, because the pasture will feed the cow alone for 90 days, you can infer that *the cow eats the daily growth plus 1/90 of the accumulated growth*. Second, because the pasture will feed the cow and the goat for 45 days, then together they will eat 1/45 of the accumulated growth. Because we inferred earlier that the *cow will eat the daily growth plus 1/90 of the accumulated growth*, then the goat will eat 1/45 - 1/90 = 1/90 of the accumulated growth each day. Third, because the pasture will feed the cow and the goose 60 days, then together they will eat 1/60 of the accumulated growth each day, of which the cow is eating 1/90 (see above). Hence, the goose will eat 1/60 - 1/90 = 1/180 of the accumulated growth each day.

To summarize, we have now established that the cow will eat the daily growth plus 1/90 of the accumulated growth each day, the goat will eat 1/90 of the accumulated growth each day, and the goose will eat 1/180 of the accumulated growth each day. Doing a bit of arithmetic we can determine that together the three animals will eat 1/90 + 1/90 + 1/180 = 1/36 of the accumulated growth each day, plus the cow will eat the daily growth. Therefore, we can now conclude that the pasture will feed all three animals for 36 days.

Change Partners

This is an interesting problem because it is most easily solved by using two tables for recording information (one for mates and another for dancing partners). From the givens you know that Betty and Ed are dancing together, and you can infer that neither is dancing with anyone else. Furthermore, you can infer that Dorothy is married to Ed, and therefore neither is married to anyone else. You can also infer that Betty is not married to George. The interesting aspect of this problem is that you can use information from the givens and from the partners matrix to infer further information about mates. Then you can use that information about mates and the givens to infer more about dancing partners. You can continue in this fashion until the problem is solved. The mates are Ed and Dorothy, Frank and Carol, George and Alice, and Harry and Betty. The dancing partners are Ed and Betty, George and Dorothy, Frank and Alice, and Harry and Carol.

Chapter 3

Ten Floor Lamps

This problem really doesn't lend itself to guided trial and error, and so you must resort to some form of systematic trial and error to solve it. It is also different from the other problems, because it tends to be more of a visual problem. It could also be considered a mental set problem because you must do something that is not obvious at first. A clue is that the number of lamps (ten) is not evenly divisible by the number of walls (four). However, a good place to start is to draw a diagram of a room and distribute an even number of lamps to each wall (two). Then with a little creativity and some trial and error, you can find a way to distribute the two remaining lamps in a way that satisfies the conditions given. One solution is shown in the accompanying illustration.

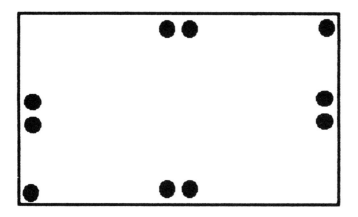

Moving Checkers

The most effective way to represent this problem is to draw some squares and use checkers or coins or something else that could be moved around. Although this problem might appear at first to be an example of random trial and error, there are some aspects that lend themselves to guided trial and error. For example, a first move should at least put two checkers of the same color together. Another consideration is not to allow too large a gap to occur between any sets of checkers. For purposes of explanation, number the checkers 1 through 6 starting at the left. Thus the leftmost checker is 1 and the rightmost one is 6. To solve the problem, first move checkers 2 and 3 to the left of 1. Then move checkers 5 and 6 left into the gap left by 2 and 3, which puts all the dark checkers together and the light checkers at the ends. Now move the two light checkers from the right end over to the left end, and the problem is solved. There is, of course, a "mirror image" solution that begins by moving checkers 4 and 5 to the right of 6.

Weighing the Baby

Many people experience difficulty in analyzing the givens to establish the relationships among the elements of this problem. They have particular difficulty interpreting the phrase "the dog weighs 60 percent less than the baby." This statement means that the dog's weight is the baby's weight minus 60% of the baby's weight. This could be represented symbolically as $D = B - .60B$, which is equivalent to $D = .40B$. The latter representation seems easier for most people to understand. The statement "She weighs 100 pounds more than the baby and the dog together" also causes problems for some people. This statement, plus the statement that all three weigh 170 pounds, plus come careful thinking should produce the inference that Mrs. O'Toole weighs 135 pounds. Therefore, the dog and the baby together weigh 35 pounds.

The two relationship that can now be used with guided trial and error to solve the problem are: (1) $D = .40B$, and (2) $D + B = 35$. A wise first choice for values should consider that relationship 1 indicates the dog weighs only two-fifths as much as the baby. The solution is that the baby weighs 25 pounds, the dog weighs 10 pounds and Mrs. O'Toole weighs 135 pounds.

Settling the Bill

This problem is a straightforward application of guided trial and error. As stated in the givens, there are two conditions that must be met. The first involves the original group that went in for the snack, and it can be represented as $M \times A = \$6$, where M equals the number of men in the group and A equals the amount each owed. After the two "freeloaders" skipped out, the condition changed and can be represented as $(M - 2) \times (A + .25) = \$6$. From there it is just a matter of finding values for M and A that will meet both conditions. For a first trial, you need values that divide evenly into $6 such as N = 5 and A = $1.20, and then work from there. The correct values are N = 8, and A = $.75.

Three Brides

This is an interesting problem because it has two parts, both of which could be solved by trial and error. The first part is the weight of the three brides. Whereas this could be solved with guided trial and error, with some careful thought you could infer the ladies' weights. Because they differ successively by 10 pounds, you can let Minnie give 10 pounds to Kitty (temporarily), and they will all weigh 132 pounds (396/3). Then you can let Kitty give the 10 pounds back to Minnie, resulting in Kitty, Nellie, and Minnie weighing 122, 132, and 142 pounds respectively.

The second part of the problem is to match the three grooms' weights with those of the three brides so that total equals 1000 pounds as stated. There really doesn't seem to be a way to choose a best first set of values for this problem, so you can try something like heaviest groom (relative to his bride) with lightest bride and lightest groom with heaviest bride. This puts Charles with Kitty, John with Millie, and William with Nellie. If you were to do this, you would find that the total weight is less than the required 1000 pounds. This should signal you to look for a combination that will increase the total, such as heaviest groom with heaviest bride and lightest groom with lightest bride. As it turns out, this latter matching scheme is the solution, with the couples being Kitty and John, Nellie and William, and Millie and Charles.

Trading Chickens

As with the Three Brides Problem, this problem has two parts, each of which can be solved with guided trial and error. The first part is to establish the worth of a cow and a horse in terms of chickens. From the givens, the two relationships to be used are (1) a cow and a horse are worth eighty-five chickens, $H + C = 85$; and (2) five horses are worth twelve cows, $5H = 12C$. Essentially, this means that you need to break 85 into two parts such that one part (to go with horses) is a little more than twice as large as the other part (to go with cows). Therefore, you should begin with numbers such as 65 and 20, test to see if these numbers give the same value when one is multiplied by 12 and the other is multiplied by 5, and then adjust as necessary. The answer to this part is that a horse is worth sixty chickens and a cow is worth twenty-five chickens.

The second part of the problem is to determine the number of horses and cows that corresponds to the relationships given as the farmer and his wife discuss the number of additional horses and cows to acquire following their initial purchases. The wife's proposal results in the relationship $2H + C = 17$; whereas the husband's proposal produces the relationship $H + 2C = 19$. The task now is to use guided trial and error to find values for H and C that satisfy both relationships. Inspection of the relationships indicates that both require that the numbers of horses and cows purchased originally were about the same. Thus, a good first guess constrained by the wife's proposal would be $H = 6$ and $C = 5$. The actual values turn out to be $H = 5$ and $C = 7$. Because the husband's proposal uses all the chickens, the number of chickens they brought to market is 5 horses × 60 chickens per horse = 300 chickens plus 14 cows × 25 chickens per cow = 350 chickens, giving a total of 650 chickens.

Sharing Apples

This is one of the more difficult problems for a couple of reasons. First, the relationships among the problem elements are kind of tricky to tease out of the givens. Second, there are three simultaneous conditions that must be satisfied to solve the problem, instead of only two as in most of the other problems. If you let S be the number of original shares and N be the number of apples in each original share, then Michael's proposal to share by families can be represented as total apples = $(N + 3) \times (S - 2)$. Fred's proposal to include himself and go back to shares by individuals can likewise be represented as total apples = $(N - 1) \times (S + 1)$. Thus, we now have two conditions.

The third condition that must be met comes from inferring that because Fred got an apple from each of the boys resulting in equal shares, then $N = S + 1$. You will find that the only values that will satisfy these three conditions are $N = 9$ and $S = 8$, giving a total of 72 apples. If you begin with sets of numbers smaller or larger than 9 and 8, you can easily converge to the solution with guided trial and error.

Wolf, Goat, and Cabbage

You probably recognized this as a detour problem, similar to the Missionaries and Cannibals Problem discussed in the chapter. It is a bit simpler, however. It is a matter of making certain that the goat doesn't have an opportunity to eat the the cabbage and that the wolf doesn't have an opportunity to eat the goat. Thus, one solution is to take the goat across the river and leave it. Then you can take either the wolf or the cabbage across, leave it, and *take the goat back*. This is where the detour is involved. You must take the goat back to the beginning side in order to prevent something from being eaten. Then take the remaining item across the river, leave it, and go back for the goat.

CHAPTER 4

Printer's Ink

This is a fairly simple application of the use of sub-goals. The sub-goals are to find the number of pages requiring various sizes of numbers (*e.g.*, single-digit pages, double-digit pages, etc.). Pages 1-9 use 9 digits, pages 10-99 use 180 digits, and pages 100-999 use 2700 digits for a cumulative total of 2889 digits. Because there are only 100 digits remaining, and they each require four digits, there can be 25 additional pages for a total of 1024.

The Mongolian Railway System

This problem is relatively simple with sub-goals defined as putting twenty-five cars at a time on the siding and "sliding" them past one another in turn until the two trains have completely passed each other. It is very helpful to draw a diagram for the track and siding and to use some objects for the parts of the train that can be moved around on the diagram.

Grundy's Game

The use of sub-goals in this problem comes in taking each of the possible moves (divisions) that the first person could make (6-1, 5-2, and 3-4) and pursuing them with additional potential moves that could be made on subsequent plays. It is useful to represent the problem in a tree diagram with each of the divisions by the first player as main branches, and their division as secondary branches, etc. There is the potential for the player going second to always win, *if* wise choices are made on the second and subsequent moves. If the first player divides the pile 6-1, then the second player must divide the 6 into 4-2, and then just follow all legal moves from there. If the first player divides 5-2, the second player must divide the 5 into 4-1 and follow legal moves from there. If the first player divides 4-3, then the second player wins just by pursuing legal moves from there.

A Train Encounter

The use of sub-goals in this problem involves dividing the two trains into forty-car segments, alternately pushing them onto the siding, pushing the other train's cars past, then moving from the siding down the track in the desired direction until the job is done. It is very helpful to draw a diagram of the track and the siding and then to use some objects to represent the various parts of the train that can be moved around on the diagram. The complete solution is shown in the accompanying illustration, wherein NE symbolizes the northbound engine, SE the southbound engine, N-40 a set of forty cars of the northbound train, and S-40 a set of forty cars of the southbound train.

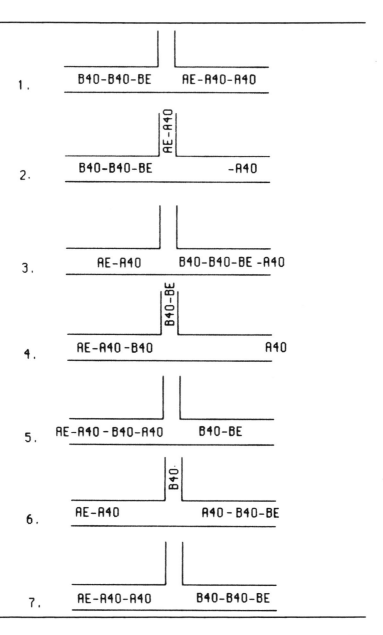

A Switching Puzzle

The sub-goals relevant to the problem are actually suggested by the way the problem is presented. That is, one sub-goal is to reverse the positions of the cars in whichever way possible and then to determine a way to do so and still return the engine to its original place and direction. Both sub-goals may require a bit of trial and error to solve. Referring to Figure 4.14, where the puzzle was presented originally, the steps to accomplish the goal with the top siding are as follows: (1) Move the white car (W) up to D and push it to B; (2) pull the black car (B1) down past and leave it; (3) move the engine around through the tunnel, pull W off B and push both cars to A; (4) take the engine back around through the tunnel and push W onto C; (5) pull B1 back to A; (6) take the engine back around through the tunnel, pull W off C, and push it to D; and (7) move the engine back to its original position at C.

The steps to accomplish the goal without the top siding are as follows: (1) Move W to the tunnel; (2) get B1 and move it to C; (3) take the engine around through the tunnel and push W past A toward D; (4) pull B1 off C, hook it to W, and push W to C; (5) leave B1 at the tunnel and go around and pull white to A; (6) push W around to D; (7) bring the engine back and move B1 to A; and (8) move the engine to its original position at C.

Routes

These problems are examples of recursive sub-goals and are similar to the Amaze Problem discussed in the chapter. The solution for Map 1 is A, B, C, D and H = 1; E = 2; F and I = 3; G = 4; J = 6; and K = 10. For Map 2: A = 1, B = 2, C = 3, D = 5, E = 8, F = 13, G = 21, H = 34, I = 55. For Map 3: A, C, G, E, and I = 1; B = 3; D = 5; F = 7; and H = 9. For Map 4: A = 2, B = 4, C = 8, and D = 16.

CHAPTER 5

Truth and Falsehood

This is a straightforward example of the use of contradiction. Probably the most difficult part of the problem is correctly interpreting and understanding the statements of the individuals described in the givens. Once that is accomplished, it is simply a matter of considering the two alternatives one at a time (the third person is either a Anania or a Diogene) and testing each against the givens. The contradiction arises when you assume the third person is a liar. If you are careful in checking the implications, you will find that this implies that the first person claims to be a liar. However, a person from neither tribe could claim to be a liar. Truth-tellers would claim to be truth-tellers because they must tell the truth, and liars would claim to be truth-tellers because they must lie.

I've Been Poisoned

This problem is very similar to those discussed in the chapter. You must proceed to assume each person, in turn, is guilty, while keeping in mind the restriction that one statement from each person is false. Because the waiter is implicated, you should also assume he did it and test. If you are careful in your reasoning, you will find that O'Neil is the culprit.

A Crime Story

This problem can be solved by assuming each person, in turn, is guilty, and testing for contradictions with the given information as discussed in the chapter. Interestingly enough, the process can be short-cut in this case because of the particular statements made by the individuals. Notice that each person, except Judy, claims not to have taken the purse and claims that someone else did. Thus, as each person is assumed to be guilty, both of those statements become false. This immediately creates a contradiction with the given that two statements of each person are true. In any event, you should find that Judy is the guilty party.

Vice Versa

Although this problem is solved using a combination of inference and contradiction, one aspect that can create difficulties for some people is that it does require you to consider the results of arithmetic operations such as borrowing and carrying. It is helpful to develop a way to record the digits that are being matched with particular letters as you proceed. One fact that can be inferred from the givens is that $E < N$. This is true because $E - N$ leaves E in the leftmost column of the answer rather than S. If E were $=$ or $> N$, S would simply be carried into the answer. This also implies that there is a borrow from S, which further implies that $N > O$, or the subtraction wouldn't have required a borrow.

Further reasoning from the information will establish that $S = E + 1$, $N - E > 1$ and that $I = H - 1$. From here, you must assume some values for N, E, and S with those constraints, and then compute values for the remaining letters that do not lead to contradictions. If you begin with $E = 1$, $S = 2$, and $N = 4$, you will find values for the other letters of $G = 8$, $H = 7$, $I = 6$, $T = 3$, and $V = 5$ that will produce one of the solutions. The other solution is $E = 4$, $S = 5$, $N = 6$, $I = 7$, $H = 8$, $V = 1$, $T = 2$, and $G = 3$.

Three Boys

This is an interesting problem in that some good tables for representing the information and some very careful inference will allow you to establish that the barefoot boy is either Chuck or Bill. From there it is a matter of contradiction. If you assume that Chuck is barefoot, then he weighs 90 pounds and Art weighs 55 pounds. If you assume that Bill is barefoot, then Chuck weighs 120 pounds and Art weighs only 25 pounds. Although the latter alternative is possible, it is not very probable because the average two-year-old weighs at least 25 pounds. Thus the more reasonable answer, given the context of the problem, is that Chuck is barefoot.

Wire Money

Of course this problem is very similar to the Vice Versa Problem, except that it involves addition rather than subtraction. It requires you to reflect on the properties of arithmetic just as does the Vice Versa Problem. Furthermore, it is similar in that you can determine values for some of the letters, and then you must resort to the method of contradiction to find the others. This problem differs further in that there are five acceptable solutions instead of two.

Because there is one more digit in the answer than in the two values added, you can infer that there is a carry from the leftmost column and that the carry could only result in M = 1. By continuing to draw inferences from the givens, you can determine that W = 9, O = 0, and Y is an even digit. From there you must assume different values for the remaining letters until you find combinations that do not lead to contradictions. The five sets of values for the other letters that produce acceptable solutions are: (1) I = 7, N = 8, R = 6, E = 2, Y = 4; (2) I = 2, N = 3, R = 8, E = 7, Y = 4; (3) I = 2, N = 3, R = 7, E = 4, Y = 8; (4) I = 5, N = 6, R = 7, E = 4, Y = 8; (5) I = 5, N = 6, R = 8, E = 7, Y = 4.

Fathers and Sons

This problem is an interesting mix of inference and contradiction. First, it is helpful to have three tables for recording the information —one for wives and husbands, one for wives and sons, and one for fathers and sons. After recording the information given in the first two statements, you must use the method of contradiction by assuming the information given in statement 3. Assuming that Allan's father is Cutler and assuming that Allan's father is Drake both lead to contradictions. This generates additional information from which you can draw further inferences relevant to the solution. Further on, you must assume the information given in statement 4, but that also leads to a contradiction. Eventually you should find that the families are (1) Louise, Barber, and Allan, (2) Dorothy, Cutler, and Henry, and (3) Beth, Drake, and Victor.

CHAPTER 6

Three Sailors and a Monkey

The smallest number of coconuts that could have been left in the morning is obviously four—one for each of the sailors and one for the monkey. Thus, this is the place to begin. The part of the problem that presents difficulty for many people is understanding that the number of coconuts left over after each sailor divided them in the night results from two equal piles having been combined. Thus, the number present before that division would be one and a half times that number plus the one given to the monkey. It must also be an even number. Thus, if you begin with four you will find that when you work backward to the third sailor you will have a total of seven, which is not an even number.

Because you have to try several values before you find one that will work backward through all three sailors, the problem also involves some systematic trial and error. You can solve the problem by starting with three piles of seven plus one for the monkey as the final division in the morning. This gives a total of twenty-two. Working backward through each sailor's division yields a total of thirty-three for the third, fifty-two for the second, and seventy-nine for the first. That is, there were at least seventy-nine coconuts gathered by the three during the day.

Trained Pigeon

It is not necessary to work backward on this problem, but it is a helpful approach to it. If you first think of the trains colliding, and then go back one hour, you will find that the trains were 60 miles apart. This, in turn, allows you to infer that if they began 120 miles apart, they must have traveled for two hours before colliding. Because the bird was traveling at 75 miles per hour for that two hours, it would have traveled 150 miles.

Guru

This is an interesting problem because so many people immediately infer that because the guru covers a net distance of 1 foot per day, it will take him 30 days to travel the necessary 30 feet. However, if you work backward from the last day, you will be able to infer that he never slips back 2 feet because he escapes. Thus, whenever he is within 3 feet of the top, he will escape the next day. Because it requires 27 days to get within 3 feet of the top, he will escape on the 28th day.

The Woolworth Game

It is almost imperative to get some checkers, coins, or other suitable objects that can be moved on some squares. If you begin with a winning position and work backward from there, you will find that the first person to move against an opponent will always lose, if the opponent takes advantage of it. That is, if one opponent closes on one set of checkers, the other opponent should close on the second set. This will require the opponent who closed first to begin retreating, and then it's just a matter of time until he loses. Therefore, a winning strategy is one that makes an opponent the first to close.

The way to avoid getting in a position where your opponent can force you to close is to establish positions so that you are separated from your opponent exactly the same number of squares on both sets of checkers. After all, that is the condition when someone has won. After establishing the same separation with both sets, you simply move to maintain the same separation until your opponent is forced to close. You can establish the necessary separation by being first and moving on the top row so that you are separated from your opponent by three squares as on the bottom. Then, if your opponent moves to within one square on either top or bottom, you move the other set to within one. At some point your opponent will be forced to close. If you are second, you can still win if your opponent allows you the opportunity to establish an equal separation on both sets of checkers.

Truck in the Desert

This problem is a very good example of the power of working backward. As you begin to work backward from the destination, you should realize that the last dump can be established 180 miles from the destination, because the truck will go that far with a full load of gas. At this point, you can begin to think about sub-goals, because the problem is just too complex to think through as a whole. The first sub-goal is to determine where to establish the second-to-the-last dump and how much gas would be needed there in order to be able to have 180 gallons at the last dump.

The number of gas dumps and the distance between them is constrained by the capacity of the truck. Obviously, the dumps must be fewer than 90 miles apart if you are to get from one to the next, dump some gas, and make it back. The smaller the distance between dumps, the more there will have to be. Because the distance from the last dump to the start is 220 miles, three additional dumps could be established 55 miles apart and with the first one 55 miles from the start. Then you can continue working backward from the last dump to determine the amount that would be needed at each previous dump. Finally, of course, you will work back to the start, and you will know how much the whole trip will require.

An important point to consider is that you don't actually need 180 gallons at the last (fourth) dump, because you can fill up at the third dump and use only 55 gallons getting to the last one. Therefore you need only 55 gallons at the last dump to finish filling the truck to the 180-gallon capacity. The same is true of the previous dumps. If you follow the same process through all dumps, you will find that you need 55 gallons at the last dump, 220 gallons at the third dump, 715 gallons at the second dump, 1980 gallons at the first dump, and 5350 gallons at the start to complete the journey. In this case, you will also determine the number of trips between each set of dumps to transport the necessary gas.

Nim

By working backward from a win, you should see that you can win by leaving your opponent with only one coin. As you work backward further, you will find that this can be accomplished by making certain that on your previous move you leave your opponent with at least five coins. That way your opponent cannot leave you with a single coin. Another important point in analyzing the game is that you can always make certain that at least four coins will be taken in a pair of moves by you and your opponent because one, two, or three coins can be taken on each move. Therefore, you can always guarantee a win by going first and taking three coins and leaving nine. Then, regardless of what your opponent does, you can take whatever you need to make certain five are left after your next move. You are then in a position to force a win on your third move.

Further Reading

Adams, J. L. *Conceptual Blockbusting*. New York: W. W. Norton & Co., 1979.

Anderson, B. *The Complete Thinker*. Englewood Cliffs, N.J.: Prentice-Hall, 1980.

Hayes, J. R. *The Complete Problem Solver*. Philadelphia: Franklin Institute Press, 1981.

McKim, R. H. *Experiences in Visual Thinking*. Monterey, Cal.: Brooks/Cole, 1972.

Runkle, G. *Good Thinking: An Introduction to Logic*. New York: Holt, Rinehart, and Winston, 1978.

Whimbey, A., & Lockhead, J. *Beyond Problem Solving and Comprehension*. Philadelphia: Franklin Institute Press, 1984.

Wickelgren, W. *How to Solve Problems*. San Francisco: Freeman & Co., 1974.

Index